Professor Cecil J. Houston is a faculty member in the University of Windsor, Ontario where he has recently completed a ten-year period as Dean of Arts and Social Sciences. Author of several papers on the Irish in Canada he is also co-author, with William J. Smyth, *The Sash Canada Wore, A Historical Geography of the Orange Order in Canada* (University of Toronto Press, 1980) and *Irish Emigration and Canadian Settlement* (Ulster Historical Foundation and University of Toronto Press, 1990). A native of Co. Derry, he is a graduate of the University of Toronto where he also served as a member of the Geography Department for many years.

Professor William J. Smyth is president emeritus of National University of Ireland Maynooth where he also served as Professor of Geography for sixteen years. Over many years he has co-authored several papers and books with Cecil J. Houston in the field of Irish settlement in Canada. Recently he has also authored *Toronto, The Belfast of Canada* (University of Toronto Press, 2015). Born in Co. Armagh, he is a graduate of the National University of Ireland and prior to becoming the first professor of Geography in Maynooth he was a member of the Geography Department in the University of Toronto.

Wilson Benson, 1821–1911

From Ulster to Canada

THE LIFE AND TIMES
OF WILSON BENSON
1821–1911

Cecil J. Houston
William J. Smyth

ULSTER HISTORICAL FOUNDATION

Ulster Historical Foundation gratefully acknowledges financial support for this publication received from the Faculty of Arts and Social Sciences, University of Windsor, Ontario, Canada.

FRONT COVER
Emigrant Ship Leaving Belfast (1852)
James Glen Wilson, 1827–1863
© National Museums Northern Ireland
Collection Ulster Museum

BACK COVER
Imperial Federation, Map of the World Showing Extent of the British Empire
by Walter Crane
http://maps.bpl.org/id/M8682/
Licensed under Public Domain via Wikimedia Commons

Brockville (Ontario) *c*. 1841, from the opposite side of the river
by Frederick H. Holloway
COURTESY OF TORONTO PUBLIC LIBRARY

First published 2015
by Ulster Historical Foundation
49 Malone Road, Belfast BT9 6RY
www.ancestryireland.com
www.booksireland.org.uk

© Cecil J. Houston and William J. Smyth
ISBN: 978-1-909556-33-1

Printed by W&G Baird Ltd.
Cover design by Dunbar Design
Text formatting by FPM Publishing

Contents

Acknowledgements

The significance of Wilson Benson's autobiography has been recognised by several Canadian scholars over the past forty years and in selected segments it has appeared in diverse works on Ontarian settlement history. Understandably, those studies interrogated Benson's writings and interpreted them within the context of the apparently completed life of a fifty-five-year-old man (1821–76). Through field and archival researches the present authors became aware that Wilson Benson's life continued for another thirty-five years and it became apparent to us that, when interpreted in its totality, his life was demonstrably different from that portrayed by earlier scholars. In particular, concepts of mobility and transiency, which had a significance when applied to the period of his life covered by the autobiography, were of much less significance when analysed in the context of a man who spent virtually all of his first twenty years in a single parish in pre-famine Ulster and his final fifty-eight years in a corner of Grey County, Ontario. His autobiography is an astute and reflective chronicle of a personal journey that spanned two sides of the Atlantic, extending in temporal sweep from the shadows of the Napoleonic era, through famine and mass migration, to a time when the structural skeleton of the Titanic was being laid in his home city, Belfast. Interpreted in the light of the totality of his life and times, the autobiography of Wilson Benson has much to offer those interested in the settlement geography and history of both Ulster and Ontario.

Wilson Benson grew up in Co. Armagh, the heartland of the Irish rural linen industry, and his prescient account of local social and economic conditions provides valuable insights into a domestic craft industry on the cusp of industrial transformation. To date, the autobiography remains largely unknown to Irish researchers. The present authors have drawn upon it for their previous study of Irish emigration to Canada, but the significance of the publication in its totality remains unrecognised in the homeland of its author. The present publication will address this lacuna for academic researchers and also provide access to what is an important contextual document for those interested in family history in both Ireland and Canada.

Many people have assisted with the completion of the present publication. Blanche Quigley, then owner of the farm homesteaded by Wilson Benson, assisted early fieldwork in Grey County. Her recall of details of the original house on the property was invaluable. Joseph Leydon, now a professor in the University of Toronto, assisted with enthusiastic and capable archival research during his time as a graduate student. Professor Tom McIlwraith generously provided the authors with unpublished research into the significance of ballast in the era of the sailing ship and was always a font of encouragement. Descendants of Wilson Benson, Rebecka Balsdon and Ted Benson, facilitated our enquiries and generously supplied the photograph of their ancestor. Toronto Public Library provided the Holloway sketches of Brockville and we are indebted also to Dr Fiona Smyth-O'Sullivan for expertly producing the illustrations contained in the publication.

Fintan Mullan and Dr William Roulston of the Ulster Historical Foundation lent encouragement, creative energy and enthusiasm to the project. We wish also to record our appreciation of the support and encouragement provided by our respective families, and their tolerance of Wilson Benson in dinner table conversation. They will be relieved that the guest has finally gone to rest.

CECIL J. HOUSTON, WINDSOR, CANADA
WILLIAM J. SMYTH, MAYNOOTH, IRELAND

Illustrations and Tables

Introduction

In 1876 the Toronto publishing house of Hunter, Rose & Co. published a slim volume amounting to fifty-six pages entitled *Life and Adventures of Wilson Benson*.[1] Authorship was declared to be "Written By Himself". It is impossible to determine the success of the publication but, judging from the rarity of surviving original copies, it is likely that the readership was very small. However, the significance of the publication rests not in its market potential but rather in the richness and authenticity of its content, and its usefulness as a tool for historical researchers and genealogists alike.

According to his autobiography Wilson Benson was born in Belfast, Ireland, in December 1821 and at the time of the publication of his life story he was a fifty-five-year-old recently retired farmer and current owner of a general store in the Canadian village of Markdale, Grey County, Ontario. Bridging great expanses of time and distance Benson's narrative connects two very different worlds on either side of the Atlantic, each of which is portrayed and interpreted in the light of his personal experiences. With commendable detail and verifiable accuracy, the book presents valuable insights into life in Ulster during the two decades that preceded the onset of the Great Famine, sketches his experiences as a seasonal migrant in Scotland, and relates the challenges encountered in the course of emigration and settlement in Canada. Pre-famine Ulster and the Canadian province of Ontario are interwoven in a migration tale that may not be of epic proportions but is, nonetheless, revelatory as the record of one man's engagement with the relentless demands of social and economic change and the personal challenges of emigration. It also documents his acquiescence in the onset of modernity and its attendant Victorian philosophy of progress.

Its brevity notwithstanding, the autobiography represents a valuable addition to the corpus of original material that documents the nature of Irish emigration to nineteenth-century Canada. Covering pivotal periods in the history of Ireland and Canada, the autobiography conveys the experience of life in two radically different but fast changing environments. It is written not in a diary format but as a chronological discourse on the principal events and places that helped shape the author's life. For the most part his recall of dates and places is consistent and accurate but, on occasion, the vagaries of memory compress events, clouding and jumbling the detailed sequencing of some of his actions. Like all works based on memory, it is selective, but that selectivity does not in any way minimise the significance of a piece of writing that, in spite of its sparseness, is a rich repository of insight and experiential detail.[2] The style of writing is quite fluid with a commendable command of grammar and syntax, indicative of a person who had attained a reasonable standard of literacy. The author was quite proud of the limited but effective schooling that he had obtained during his youth in Co. Armagh in the 1830s and several references strewn throughout his autobiography suggest that he developed and maintained an active reading interest in the newspapers and publications of contemporary Canada.

The use of published diaries and personal narratives in historical analysis is not without controversy, and especially so with respect to Ireland–Canada migration linkages. Gerald Keegan's *Famine Diary* is a case in point.[3] Published originally in 1895 by Robert Sellar under the title *The Summer of Sorrow*, it was re-published in 1982 under the title *The Voyage of The Naparima* by James J. Mangan before it re-appeared in 1991 as a contribution to the burgeoning literature prompted by the sesquicentenary of the Irish Famine. *Famine Diary: Journey To The New World* purported to be the personal account of a Co. Sligo schoolteacher who had arrived, amid horrendous circumstances of death, disease, and starvation, in Canada in 1847. Initially accepted by many academics as an authentic historical source, the book was eventually revealed as originating in a fictional account penned by Robert Sellar for *The Huntingdon Gleaner*, a newspaper he edited in late nineteenth-century Quebec. In a similar vein, the Canadian publication, *The Yellow Briar*, which appeared in 1933, was immediately accepted as an authentic account of Irish Famine settlement and pioneer farming in the Ontarian township of Mono but it was soon discovered that the publication was a work of fiction. Its real author was a Toronto-based lawyer, John Mitchell, writing under a *nom de plume*.[4]

The professional requirement to validate the authenticity of all documents employed in historical analysis is germane to the present republication and analysis of the life and times of Benson's autobiography. An eminent and respected Toronto publishing house published the original autobiography. Founded in 1861, Hunter, Rose & Co., became the legislative printer for Canada, and following Canadian Confederation in 1867 the company signed a ten-year contract for the printing and binding of all official publications in the province of Ontario. It still retained that contract at the time of the Benson publication.[5] The reputation of the company was beyond reproach and the authenticity of Benson's book was further supported by the personal testimonials of two clergymen who may have assisted the author during his recuperation from a farm accident in

1873. There is no reason to question the authenticity of a publication that, in style and content, was quite capable of being written by a man of high intelligence and modest education. The only possible exception is the rather pretentious title page declaration:

> *"Multum in Parvo"*
> "The Divine Right of Kings is co-existent with The Author of Nature"

Either the publisher, or the two supportive clergymen, may have contributed this insertion, and its reference to Lockian philosophy.

As a further test of authenticity the factual details presented in the publication have been assessed and verified through investigation by the present authors. *Life and Adventures of Wilson Benson* contains many specific references to places and people on both sides of the Atlantic. Any fabrication of the highly personalized geography by the author would have required a challenging and improbable familiarity with a number of widely separated localities along with a detailed knowledge of their local inhabitants. With the aid of archival sources in Ireland and Canada, and augmented by fieldwork in both countries, the life-world of Benson has been authenticated, reconstructed, and explored. The range of sources employed, and the intertwining of the tools of geography and history in their analysis and application should prove of value not only to academics researching the field of migration studies but should also have relevance for the burgeoning numbers of genealogists involved in the reconstruction of family histories and personal linkages in both Ireland and Canada.

Source Materials

Sources employed in the present research are diverse in nature, potential value and relevance, and are unbalanced between the Irish and Canadian parts of Benson's life. In general, the Canadian sources are more comprehensive than those available in Ireland and, in large measure, this difference may be explained by the periodicity of the author's life, as well as by the completeness and survival of relevant material. Benson's Irish experience was pre-famine in timing (1821–41) and it predated the 1864 statutory requirement for compulsory registration of vital statistics. Data on births, marriages and deaths for the 1820s and 1830s exist in church records but these sources are incomplete and their regional coverage is uneven. The period of Benson's life in Ireland was covered by national censuses in 1821, 1831 and 1841 but only fragments of the manuscript enumerator returns have survived. An 1821 census fragment does survive for part of Kilmore parish in Co. Armagh but, unfortunately, it does not extend to the townlands of Mullantine and Bottlehill in which Benson's father had resided. Church records for Belfast, 1796–1830, were researched but no record of Wilson's birth or the death of his mother was found. Similarly, a search of parish records for north Co. Armagh failed to reveal any information for Benson and his immediate family but they did provide a birth record for his wife, Jemima Hewitt. Tithe Applotment records for the 1830s provide details for Hewitt's family but they are silent in respect to Benson's father who was living in the townland of Mullantine at that time.[6] Information from Seagoe parish's Tithe Applotment records does identify a number of Bensons living in the vicinity of Portadown and it is possible that they were part of a wider family connection.[7] The 1821 census fragment for Kilmore parish does, however, provide information for the family of William Cullen to whom Wilson was hired at the age of twelve. With the aid of post-famine land valuation records it is possible to identify localities and other individuals mentioned in the text but the detail of the information is unsatisfactory.[8] It may well be the case that the Benson family, by virtue of its geographical mobility within Ulster and rapid descent into poverty, simply fell below the radar of the existing coverage of records while, in contrast, the family background of Jemima Hewitt suggests somewhat greater stability, social standing and visibility within the local rural community.

Wilson spent half a year in Scotland, possibly in 1839, with his unnamed sister and brother-in-law and, although the brevity and timing of the Scottish sojourn precluded his appearance in any census record, there is sufficient ancillary evidence to support the veracity of details recounted by him. Specifically, the street directories for Glasgow confirm the name, address and business specialisms of the merchant from whom he obtained a quantity of small goods for peddling. Contemporary directories for Belfast verify Benson's assertion that the same merchant also had a commercial presence in the Ulster city. Post office directories for Edinburgh and its surrounding hinterland include the name and address of the farmer for whom Benson worked for a few weeks as a seasonal labourer and his return voyage to Belfast was on board a steamship that is identifiable in shipping records. His reference to a railway journey from Belfast to Lisburn, in particular, provides additional and useful information for estimating the temporal framework of his Scottish trip.

In his narrative Benson identifies the emigrant ship that he boarded in Belfast in the spring of 1841, and collaborative detail for the departure of that ship, *Sarah Stewart*, for Canada was reported by *The Belfast Newsletter* for a date very proximate to the one recorded in the autobiography. Canadian sources affirm both the departure and arrival of the ship and also confirm regular sailings of the *Sarah Stewart* from Belfast to Quebec in other years.[9] In general, the Canadian source materials are much more rewarding than their Irish counterparts, especially for the post 1850 period. A Quebec newspaper verified the arrival of the *Sarah Stewart*, documented the number of its passengers and noted the duration of the period spent reloading the ship in the Canadian port. Local records identify the Brockville hotel in which Benson found early employment and Toronto taxation records provide evidence of his occupancy of a store in that city in 1846. Thereafter a range of other official documents captures the social and geographical mobility of the immigrant. A church record for 1862 provides details of his second marriage and it is from this document that we discover, for the first time, the names of his mother and father who by that time had died in Ireland. Canadian manuscript census material for a total of seven censuses in the period 1851–1911 provides detailed demographic data for the Benson family as well as collaborative information on persons mentioned in the course of the narrative. It was the era of officialdom in Canada and that approach was extended in 1863 to include compulsory registration of all Canadian births, deaths and marriages – thereby providing evidence of the entirety of the second half of Benson's life.

The nature of the settlement process in Canada involved the issuance of land patents and mortgage documentation. These sources, in addition to contemporary cadastral maps and historical atlases, provide detailed geographical evidence of Wilson Benson's location on the rural frontier. In addition, the success and nature of his farming ventures may be ascertained from decennial agricultural records. Other less official, but nonetheless informative sources, augment the census and property valuation records. The latter part of the nineteenth century saw the emergence of cheap methods of mass printing, and local newspapers were seized upon by local communities not only as a means of publicizing local, national and international news but also as a statement of urban progress and civic ambition. *The Markdale Standard* commenced publication in 1880 and for the next three decades it carried weekly adverts of the merchandise on sale in Benson's store. It published occasional accounts of events with which his family were connected and, ultimately, it carried obituary notices for Agnes and Wilson Benson in 1908 and 1911 respectively, and for some of their children subsequently. His probated will testifies to the property owned by him at his death and in the pattern of dispersal of assets it reveals, for our interpretation, much about Benson's enduring relationship with the children of his two marriages.

His Canadian life was lived in a different era and country and the evident improvement in record keeping and the publication of details of individuals collapsed the borders between personal and public, and voluntary and statutory information in the recording of data. It is a process that has continued with increased coverage into the present digital era. Within the context of that digital era and the emergence of web searches and *Ancestry.com* a new element has become available for the authentication of the Benson story. Benson's descendants have initiated genealogical searches for details of their great grandfather and have shared findings with the present authors.

Significance of the Autobiography

The significance of the autobiography for the reconstruction of society and culture in Ireland and Canada is considerable; all the more so because it was written by a man of a modest and low social profile. Benson's personal sketch of his life is especially important given that it is an articulate and experiential rendition of the unfolding settlement geography of early Ontario. Publication of his account was preceded by those of several well-known witnesses from the polite upper echelons of nineteenth-century society. The sisters Susanna Moodie and Catherine Parr Traill, as well as their brother Samuel Strickland, are well-known nineteenth-century commentators on the themes of surviving in Canada.[10] From their own privileged perspectives they describe the opportunities, disappointments and unexpected privations of life on the frontier and their writings were used subsequently in contemporary emigration propaganda. Susanna Moodie's highly popular *Roughing It in the Bush*, containing a personal account of pioneer life in Ontario in the 1830s, was first published in London in 1852, but a Canadian edition did not appear until 1871. However, it may be surmised that Benson was aware of it as he cites in parenthesis the expression "Roughing it in the Bush".[11] Unlike the Moodies, Benson was never a leader in society; neither he, Jemima, nor his second wife Agnes Shield, accumulated immense wealth. In 1876, they possessed little more than the proceeds of the farm that they had pioneered and sold for $3,000 and when Benson died in 1911 he left only a very modest inheritance to his children.

In another vein, however, and because of the accuracy and perceptiveness of his account, Benson has achieved a degree of considerable importance within the historiography of nineteenth-century Ontario. For many professional historians he has become much more than a footnote in history. As one Canadian historian has noted, Benson's brief autobiography presents "more authentic social history than most scholars have produced in volumes four or five times that size".[12]

During the 1970s, an emergent Canadian labour history movement adopted Benson's autobiography as a touchstone for assessing the significance of population mobility in shaping Ontario society. Young historians tackled key historical questions about class, inequality and social structures, by delving into the records of individuals in the nineteenth-century censuses. They developed facility with quantitative methods of matrix and demographic analysis that could assess multiple variables and hundreds of thousands of pieces of data. They created complex cross tabulations with which to compare social frameworks and describe communities, harnessing for the first time the capabilities of computer spreadsheets and statistical techniques. Through their efforts, the new historians injected a strong social aspect to the traditional political emphasis of Canadian history. Information sources that had been used previously by genealogists and biographers to track individual people were now mined to provide perspectives on large populations and complex community structures.

The most complete demonstration of this approach to historical analysis, and one that directly involved Benson's autobiography, was undoubtedly a study published by Michael Katz in 1975 entitled *The People of Hamilton, Canada West: Family and Class in a Mid-nineteenth Century City*.[13] He analysed the social structure of the Ontarian city of Hamilton by collating and interlinking the census and tax assessment information for every person living in the city in 1851 and 1861. He discovered that about a third of the people of Hamilton in 1851 were no longer living in the city ten years later: they had simply moved on to places unknown. Upon this basis, he argued that transiency characterized much of the city's society, reflecting the prevailing uncertainty of economic possibilities.

To exemplify the ways by which transiency arose in the emerging industrial city, Katz turned from his statistical analysis to include the very personal story of Benson. He thereby introduced Benson to the world of Canadian historiography.[14] The historian had discovered Benson's little volume quite by chance, almost a century after it was written, while browsing in the Robarts Library at the University of Toronto. He presented an interpretation of *Life and Adventures* as an illustration of the nature of rootlessness and transiency in mid-nineteenth century Ontario. Referencing an intensive analysis of the details of the turns and twists of Benson's journey from Co. Armagh in Ireland to the town of Markdale in Canada. Katz argued that:

> The wandering, fluctuating search for success that led Wilson Benson through Ireland, Scotland, and Upper Canada as he tried his hand at a variety of tasks from weaving and peddling to porridge-making, storekeeping and farming marked, if my speculations are correct, the lives of many men. Though their specific experiences took many forms, shaped by culture, origin and especially by accident, the transiency and uncertain attempt to climb the ladder of fortune were central themes in the lives of nineteenth century people.[15]

It is an attractive argument but the precise relevance of Benson must be evaluated against the factual background that, apart from a few months spent in Kingston and Toronto in the mid-1840s, Benson never really experienced a prolonged period of urban industrial living. The greater part of his life was lived in rural and small town communities and he was never a resident of Hamilton.

By his own admission, Benson had experience of thirty different jobs during his lifetime but virtually all of that employment history and its associated geographical mobility were concluded by the time he was thirty years of age. Most of his jobs were of short duration. Some of them lasted only a few days; others did not extend beyond a few months. Apart from a prolonged weaving apprenticeship in Ireland, none of his employment extended beyond one year until he took up farming in 1849 at the age of twenty-eight. Thereafter his life was much more settled. He farmed his first holding in Amaranth Township, Wellington County, Ontario for two or three years before moving about seventy kilometres northwards to Grey County and Artemesia Township. It was his penultimate move and he remained there for the next twenty-one years. Indeed, when injury forced him to abandon farming in 1874, his final move to Markdale involved a journey of about two kilometres and he remained in that town until his death in 1911 – thirty-five years after the publication of his autobiography.

In their totality, the overall geographical dimensions of his life reflect a relatively settled profile, notwithstanding his transatlantic migration and subsequent westward moves over distances of hundreds of kilometres in Canada. Apart from a half year spent in Scotland, Benson spent the first twenty years of his life within a few kilometres' radius of his father's home in Co. Armagh. Indeed some of his early experiences as domestic servant and apprentice were in the homes of neighbours who resided less than a kilometre from his home. In Canada the final fifty-eight years of his life were spent in two homes separated by no more than two kilometres. In summary, seventy-eight years of his ninety-year lifespan were spent in two small localities, albeit more than several thousand kilometres apart, and the rootedness of that life rather than the mobility and multiplicity of jobs characteristic of the decade of his twenties is a more accurate descriptor of his life. His period of transiency may be correlated with life cycle events and a particular period in his family formation. His story was about persistence not transience. He had spent only twelve years getting from Armagh to the vicinity of Markdale; much of his transiency was compressed into those years and thereafter his life was much more settled.

Katz's supplementary argument that Benson was "premodern [lacking] the calculating discipline that subservience to time, large work settings and technology have imposed on the modern man"[16] also sits somewhat at variance with the unfolding details of the migrant's life. In Ireland, Benson lived on the cusp of massive social and economic change caused by the implosion of the traditional craft occupation of linen spinning and weaving, the associated emergence of a complex industrial system and a contemporaneous collapse of the local agricultural economy. In Canada, after opportunistic engagement in an array of short-term jobs, he turned to frontier farming, despite the fact that little in his background prepared him for life as an agriculturalist. In the process he learned much about adopting new technology to the challenges posed by land clearance, house building and farming on a rapidly changing agricultural frontier. During the final thirty-five years of his life he earned his living as a general merchant, drawing upon earlier experiences as a peddler and purveyor of whiskey. He imported a broad range of manufactured goods from Britain and Ireland, and later from the newly settled Northwest Territories, retailing them to the residents of the village of Markdale and its surrounding hinterland. His willingness to engage with new trends and to embrace new opportunities typified a life that was profoundly steeped in a ready acceptance of the cultures of progress and modernity.

Born a few months prior to the death of Napoleon Bonaparte, he lived through and beyond the reign of Queen Victoria and died only a few months before an Atlantic iceberg sank the Belfast-built *Titanic*. Benson witnessed social and material change on a grand scale and he engaged with it in a relentless and positive (if sometimes unsuccessful) manner. The geography of his life is comprehensible as the outcome of a man seeking to do what he knew and learning from what he did not. He made numerous mistakes and encountered his share of bad luck, but for a man who had no savings and few skills when he and his wife arrived in Canada, he survived the challenge of settlement, produced and supported two families and saw them attain considerable success in their own lives before his death at the age of ninety.

Benson's stated purpose was that his autobiography might help "preserve, from oblivion and the ashes of the past, a sketch which might serve future generations in the compilation of a future History of Western Canada (Ontario)".[17] This functional imperative was not unique among the genre of other contemporary amateur historians in English Canada. Toronto historian, Carl Berger, has identified a trend towards establishing local historical societies in post-Confederation Canada and the popularity of themes of material progress and improvement that typified their publications.[18] Benson was tremendously proud of the progress and achievements that had been registered by his fellow Ontarians and he unambiguously proclaimed himself a committed Canadian. The immigrant had ceased to be a restless spirit. He was comfortable with his new life and with considerable satisfaction he asserted "Looking upon the history of one's country as an heirloom, to be preserved at all hazards, has been the chief incentive to my taking up my pen, in my humble way in that behalf."[19]

A further goal inspired the writing of the autobiography. Benson upheld the details of his life as a personal morality tale stating "I have exhibited my own life, with all its imperfections, as a guide to the reader in the path of his own journey through life."[20] Life, he emphasized, should be directed towards the pursuit of honour and truth, and by that argument he posits a sense of transcendence. However, this didactic assertion sits at some remove from the more factual rendition of the details of his life that characterize the greater part of his autobiography.

Overall his narrative is strikingly short on details of the maturation of personal and family relationships. The names and the fate of his many children and even the names of his parents and sister are absent from the text. The reader remains unclear as to whether he has one, or two, brothers-in-law living in Ontario. He omits all the domestic and family events that occurred in his home life and in his relationship with Jemima and, later, Agnes. His being regularly absent from home during the early years of his married life in the 1840s may have been a factor influencing how he perceived close relationships. He has little to say about the contributions of his wives to the family's economy or his children's role in farm and domestic chores, spinning and weaving. He does not comment on the family's attendance at the Methodist church and his own at the Church of England. In its general structure the autobiography pivots around a recall of places and events, the ecology of the forested landscape of Canada and the extremities of its seasonal weather. The death of Jemima, the crippling injury to his leg, the threatening presence of bears and wolves, and incidents of economic misfortune do evoke emotive comment but these examples are rare and the commentary brief. For the most part, the path of his personal odyssey is chartered by unencumbered factual detail and in that lies much of its significance. Like a well-drawn sketch, simple lines and shaded allusions may deliver great meaning. Few other sources capture with such simple elegance the travails of life, society and geographical experience of life in pre-famine Ulster and early Canada.

The autobiography was written during a period of convalescence from his farming injuries and the very severity of those injuries probably gave Benson cause to reflect on his own mortality and the directions chosen throughout his life. The period of slow painful recuperation and the ministrations of the two named clergymen may well have influenced the tone and content of the final two pages of his book. He does not appear to have written a sequel relating to his life as a shopkeeper in Markdale where he regained his health and lived for several more decades. The present authors have researched the details of that latter period of his life and have included them in this study of his life and times. Those details extend the compass of his experience by a further thirty-five years and they bring closure to the story of a life that continued to evolve and adjust to the ongoing impetus of social and economic change.

Structure of Presentation

The present study contains two distinct but related sections. In the first section the authors locate the life experiences of Benson in the wider contexts of the Irish and Canadian societies of which he was part. In so doing the autobiography is elucidated and interpreted by reference to more general forces of geographical development. By extension, the details of Benson's life are employed to inject an experiential dimension into historical studies, breathing vitality into analyses derived from summary statistical data, and expanding the historiography of Irish emigration and Canadian settlement. Through this historical evaluation the present study also assesses a range of source material that genealogists, in particular, may find useful. The second section of the study consists of a reproduction of Benson's published narrative. It is a story that has been featured in partial form in other historical studies but this publication presents it in its entirety and opens it up to a wide readership that hopefully may find inspiration to further explore the shared national and personal linkages that bind Ireland and Canada, and the cultural transfers that initiated and have maintained those linkages over many decades. The story also possesses a contemporary quality. In outlining a family's response to rapid economic change it parallels our own time's uncertain challenges for youth in the search for work that leads often to short-term employment, the frequent updating of skills, and separation from home. The two sections provide readers with an opportunity to formulate their own interpretation of Benson's *Life and Adventures*.

The reproduction of the original work is faithful to the pagination and layout of the 1876 publication. The illustrations are additional to the original work and they include a photograph of Wilson that was generously provided by his familial descendants. It depicts Wilson during the time he lived in Markdale. His clear expression and direct gaze may be fancifully interpreted as a reflection of his personality, although in reality it may be merely a contrivance of the photographer. It is the only available evidence of what Benson looked like in reality and it gives little hint of his general stature or physical presence. Comments scattered throughout his autobiography would seem to indicate that he was a person of slight build and low weight. In Scotland, for example, although he was in his late teens he was assigned, along with women and girls, to cook porridge for the field labourers. Later, in Canada, he was tossed high in the air by a bull, and in his threshing machine accident he was sufficiently slight as to fit under the revolving drive shaft. All of these incidents are but grounds for conjecture: all available evidence points to a man of tremendous energy, nerve, and ambition who was buffeted by the fortunes of life and yet lived until his ninetieth year.

Notes and References

1   The copy of Wilson Benson's autobiography used by the present authors is to be found in the Thomas Fisher Rare Books Room of the University of Toronto. Microfilm copies are located in a few other libraries, including the National Library and Archives of Canada, Ottawa. More recently the University of Alberta has published a copy in e-book format. Forgotten Books, London, also reprinted the book in 2013.

2   The use of memory in historical writing is the central focus of a growing literature in the historical and social sciences. An appropriate and excellent review of this literature is to be found in a recent work that documents twentieth century links between Northern Ireland and Canada, see Johanne Devlin Trew, *Leaving The North: Migration and Memory, Northern Ireland 1921–2011* (Liverpool: Liverpool University Press, 2013) 10–25.

3   Gerald Keegan, *Famine Diary: Journey To A New World* (Dublin: Wolfhound Press, reprinted 1991). See also J. Mangan, *The Voyage of The Naparima: A Journal of 1847* (Quebec: Carraig Books, 1982). A good account of the historiography of the debate surrounding Famine Diary is that of Jason King, "The Genealogy of Famine Diary in Ireland and Quebec: Ireland's Famine Migration in Historical Fiction, Historiography, and Memory," in *Eire-Ireland*, vol. 47, 2012, 45–69.

4   Patrick Slater, *The Yellow Briar*, (Toronto: Thomas Allen, 1933).

5   Company records pertaining to Hunter, Rose & Co. Printers are held in the Thomas Fisher Rare Books Room of the University of Toronto. These records, along with three hundred books that had been printed by the company were deposited with the university when the printing company ceased to operate in 1983. It would appear that the library's copy of Wilson Benson's autobiography predated the acquisition of the company papers.

6   Tithe Applotment records were compiled 1823–37 in order to facilitate the collection of tithes from those who occupied more than one acre of agricultural land. It is probable that the Benson family had fallen below this threshold and so do not appear in the record.

7   The Tithe Applotment book for Seagoe parish in 1834 records the presence of James Benson in the townland of Drumlisnagrilly, Jas. Benson in Drumgor, Thos. Benson in Crossmecaghley and another Thos. Benson in Lylo. A full list of the Seagoe parish residents enumerated in this source is to be found on the web page www.lurganancestry.com. Copies of the original Tithe Applotment books are held in the Public Record Office of Northern Ireland.

8 Griffith's land valuation of all properties in Co. Armagh was published in 1863; a generation after Benson had emigrated to Canada. This valuation record refers to the location of houses and amount of land held by heads of families. It contains no demographic information for other family members.

9 In the 1840s *The Quebec Mercury* was published three times per week in Quebec City and it included a regular column reporting the arrival of ships and their passenger numbers in some detail.

10 Contemporary writings of relevance to Canadian settlement during the early and mid-nineteenth century include Catherine Parr Traill, *The Canadian Settler's Guide* (Toronto: McClelland and Stewart reprinted 1969), and also by the same author, *The Backwoods of Canada* (Toronto: McClelland and Stewart reprinted 1967), Susanna Moodie, *Roughing It in the Bush* (Toronto: McClelland and Stewart reprinted 1967), Samuel Strickland, *Twenty-Seven Years Residence in Canada West* (Toronto: McClelland and Stewart, reprinted 1967).

11 Benson, Life and Adventures, 125. See also Carl P.A. Ballstadt, "Strickland, Susanna," in *Dictionary of Canadian Biography*, vol. 11, University of Toronto/University of Laval, 2003 – accessed October 9, 2014, http://www.biographi.ca/en/bio/strickland-susanna-11E.html.

12 Michael Katz, *The People of Hamilton, Canada West: Family and Class in a Mid-Nineteenth City* (Cambridge Massachusetts: Harvard University Press, 1975), 94.

13 Ibid.

14 Katz uses the example of Wilson Benson to demonstrate the nature of transiency and class fluidity within contemporary society. Katz's study of Hamilton was followed by that of David Gagan, *Hopeful Travellers: Families, Land, and Social Change in Mid-Victorian Peel County, Canada West* (Toronto: University of Toronto Press, 1981). Like Katz, Gagan also challenged assumptions of stable rural populations on the frontier. His findings revealed that half of the population recorded in one census was not in the records of the following census, ten years later. Wilson Benson's autobiography has featured also in Darrell A. Norris, "Migration, Pioneer Settlement, And The Life Course: The First families of an Ontario Township" in J.K. Johnson and Bruce G. Wilson (eds), *Historical Essays On Upper Canada; New Perspectives* (Ottawa: Carlton University Press, 1989), 175–201. A further examination of the relevance of Wilson Benson to studies of Irish geographical mobility in nineteenth-century Canada is to be found in C. J. Houston and W. J. Smyth, "Geographical Transiency and Social Mobility: The Illustrative Odyssey of Irish Immigrant Wilson Benson, A Well-Known Canadian Unknown," in *British Journal of Canadian Studies*, vol. 7, no. 2, 1992, 345–56.

15 Katz, *The People of Hamilton*, 175.

16 Ibid., 110.

17 Benson, 87.

18 Carl Berger, *The Writing of Canadian History* (Toronto: University of Toronto Press, 1974), 4.

19 Benson, 88.

20 Benson, 137.

Brockville *c.* 1841, looking down the St Lawrence River
as sketched by Frederick H. Holloway

1

Wilson Benson's Irish World: Population, Economy and Society in Pre-Famine Ireland

Prior to his departure for Canada in 1841 at the age of twenty, Wilson Benson had spent most of his childhood and early adulthood in the Co. Armagh parishes of Kilmore and Drumcree. Located to the southwest of Portadown the district was characterised by a complex rural economy in which agriculture, domestic spinning of flax yarn and the weaving of linen cloth were interdependent activities and most households existed at, or below, a modest level of subsistence. The region was generally recognised as the heartland of the Irish linen industry and his autobiography reveals many striking insights into the local society and economy in the second quarter of the nineteenth century. From the mid-eighteenth century the rural communities of north Armagh, and adjoining districts in the counties of Antrim and Down, had been shaped and defined by rapid natural population increase combined with an unusually high degree of localised in-migration. Expansion of both the domestic and export markets for Irish fine linen generated an unprecedented demand for skilled weavers. Hundreds of migrants from Tyrone and Fermanagh in west Ulster, Cavan and Monaghan in south Ulster, as well as from Louth in north Leinster moved into the linen triangle bounded by Armagh City, Lisburn and Dungannon.

In an Ireland supposedly distinguished by the rootedness and localism of its rural population the demographic flux of the linen region was highly distinctive and was indicated, *inter alia*, by a comparatively greater variety of surnames than most other parts of Ireland. A volatile combination of population pressure, competition for scarce resources, and a legacy of colonial bitterness created a backdrop of social tensions. In the context of the politico-religious geography of contemporary Ulster those tensions were routinely expressed through sectarian conflict. In 1795, a generation before Benson's birth, the Orange Order had been founded within a radius of fifteen kilometres of what were to be his childhood haunts. Much of the

1

community conflict that preceded, and followed, the formation of that organization took the form of the wrecking of looms, the burning of weavers' houses and forced evictions. Localities associated with these "Armagh outrages" would have been very familiar to the young Benson.

Demographic growth contributed to increasing difficulty for the many families whose survival from spinning and weaving required the additional supplement of gardens and small agricultural holdings. In response to the growing population pressure the size of agricultural holdings was further reduced. By the time of the 1841 census the rural population density in Kilmore parish exceeded 130 persons per square kilometre and the majority of farms dropped below five acres in size. Spades, not horse-drawn ploughs, were the agricultural implements adopted by most farmers for their miniscule plots of land. Accordingly, it was not surprising that Benson admitted to complete ineptitude as a ploughman when he obtained his first employment in Canada. At the time of his birth, Co. Armagh was the most densely populated county in Ireland. When he emigrated to Canada in 1841 he left behind an overcrowded landscape that was among the most densely settled rural areas in western Europe.[1]

Reduced access to land generated a growing, and increasingly marginalized, population of labourers who, if they were fortunate, lived in small mud walled cabins with perhaps a quarter of an acre that was used for potato cultivation. Evidence presented to the 1835 parliamentary inquiry into the condition of the poorer classes in Ireland described conditions in Kilmore parish, Co. Armagh, in terms of:

> The greater number of labourers in this neighbourhood can weave, and when not employed in the cultivation of the land they usually betake themselves to the loom: but the wages for weaving are very low, unless they can make fine cloth, and then they are good, but not the third part can weave fine work.[2]

The local economy was labour-intensive and, for generations, it had been characterised by a seasonal rhythm of alternating engagement in agricultural and linen production but by the 1830s, however, fundamental structural alterations in the process of linen production were underway. An emphasis on capital-intensive enterprises typified the new regime. Machine spinning of yarn was fast becoming a factory-based industrial process. Within little more than a decade, mechanized power looms would replace handlooms for the manufacture of all but the finest quality of linen cloth. Benson's experiences as a youth in Ulster coincided with this period of flux and he recognised that there was little future in his occupation as a handloom weaver. Eventually the new industrial order would destroy the interdependent elements of an intricately structured traditional agro-industrial economy, eliminate self-employed domestic spinners and weavers, and replace them by an urban industrial economy. Much of the seasonal and longer-term mobility that characterized Benson's life during his first decade in Canada was an extension of his experience of Ulster's economic transition. Regardless of whether he went to Canada or remained in Ireland, it is likely that his life would have included moving out of the increasingly redundant socio-economic structure in which he had spent his early years. The time and place of Benson's youth were by no means static backdrops of unchanging and isolated peasant culture: the propensity for change in Co. Armagh informed much of his subsequent behaviour as he established himself in his new home across the Atlantic.

Early Life in Ulster

Born in Belfast in 1821, Benson was brought by his recently widowed father to a farm in the townland of Drumnasue on the outskirts of Portadown when he was about a year old. This urban-to-rural migration might well appear as an inversion of the more normal migratory pattern of industrializing society but it did fit within the context of a society that was struggling to cope with change; uncertain of its magnitude and ultimate direction. In Belfast, his "father kept a weaving shop, employing a number of men" and the family would therefore appear to have been of some means. Notwithstanding its Belfast location, the weaving shop was probably similar in scale and function to many weaving sheds dotted throughout rural areas in Co. Armagh. In the northern and central part of that county small-scale merchants practised a system of putting out piecework to employee weavers who operated traditional handlooms, either in their own homes or in multi-loom weaving sheds. The capital requirements of linen production expanded significantly in the early nineteenth century. The scale of enterprises being undertaken by linen merchants, bleachers and owners of mechanized spinning factories increasingly placed small-scale operatives at a disadvantage.

Faced with the challenge of such competition the elder Benson resorted to the more traditional outlet of farming. He abandoned Belfast and returned to his roots on the edge of Portadown in Co. Armagh. It is possible that he was well acquainted with the area for the Tithe Applotment books for the neighbouring parish of Seagoe show three families of Benson living within a ten-kilometre radius in 1834.[3] Apparently he brought some capital with him for, upon marrying a widow who was facing eviction from her farm, he had sufficient means to pay off her debts and build a new house on the land. However, he failed to secure his title to the leasehold of the house and lands, and in a classic Irish squabble over inheritance he was evicted subsequently at the behest of his grown-up stepchildren. Over the

3

next few years the elder Benson moved home several times within the locality. In the process he appears to have dropped down the social ladder, possibly becoming landless. He is not identifiable in estate records or Tithe Applotment records in the 1830s and 40s and remains anonymous amid the overcrowded rural community in which he lived. His first name, John, was not revealed in his son's autobiography and it was established only by means of the marriage certificate issued in Canada to Wilson on the occasion of his second marriage in 1862.

The constrained circumstances of his father who had been "suddenly reduced to penury" led to Wilson being hired out at a young age as a servant "I was in consequence, compelled, at twelve years of age, to hire to a man named Wm. Cullen, receiving a salary of 4s. 6d. sterling for three months' service."[4] He is not specific as to his duties but they were probably those of a general servant in a household that would have been involved in both domestic linen production and agriculture. His payment of little more than four pence per week would have been supplemented by the provision of room and board with the family but conditions would have been spartan at best. As Wilson remarked "my labour was hard and treatment worse". It was a common destiny for many of his young peers.

In many parts of the country young adolescents were hired out for domestic and farm work through hiring fairs that were arranged to coincide with the commencement of the spring planting or the summer and autumn harvesting seasons. Girls, as well as boys, were hired out in this manner and although their monetary reward would have been meagre, their temporary absence meant one less mouth to feed at home. Lofts, barns and byres were the usual sleeping quarters and little attention was paid to the educational or personal welfare of the child labourers. In the case of Benson it would appear that the hiring was done by means of personal contact with neighbours who were in a position to make use of the services of the twelve-year-old boy. A surviving manuscript fragment of the 1821 census, as well as evidence from the Tithe Applotment books for the 1830s, identify a William Cullen living in the townland of Derryhale, an area that immediately adjoined the townland of Drumnasue where Wilson's father lived.[5] This Cullen was probably the employer and, if so, the young Benson would have been hired out to a family residing no more than a kilometre distant from his father's home. The social geography of the Derryhale community in 1821, the year Benson's father returned to the area from Belfast, can be reconstructed from a surviving fragment of the manuscript census for Kilmore parish, facilitating a detailed analysis of a locality that may be considered as being broadly representative of north Armagh society in general.

Derryhale townland, containing some 770 acres of moderately fertile agricultural land and 60 acres of bog, was home to 608 persons in 1821. It was a densely settled district: small farms, most of them fewer than five acres, and labourer cottages with small gardens attached were the dominant settlement types. Virtually all adults, women as well as men, were remuneratively engaged in farming and linen production. In addition, the census referred to a small number of other occupations, including a tailor, two seamstresses, a bonnet maker, several apprentices, an innkeeper, a carpenter, four shoemakers, two blacksmiths and two schoolteachers, one of whom was also a farmer. It was a remarkably self-reliant community but it was also one that, in spite of its domestic reliance on potatoes and other garden produce, was very much engaged in a wider sphere of commerce and was thereby susceptible to currents of economic change. A contemporary Ulster poet described in evocative terms the social impact of the contemporary economic transformation.

> And well may Erin weep and wail
> The day the wheels began to fail,
> Our tradesmen now can scarce get kail
> Betimes to eat,
> In shipfuls they are doomed to sail
> In quest of meat.[6]

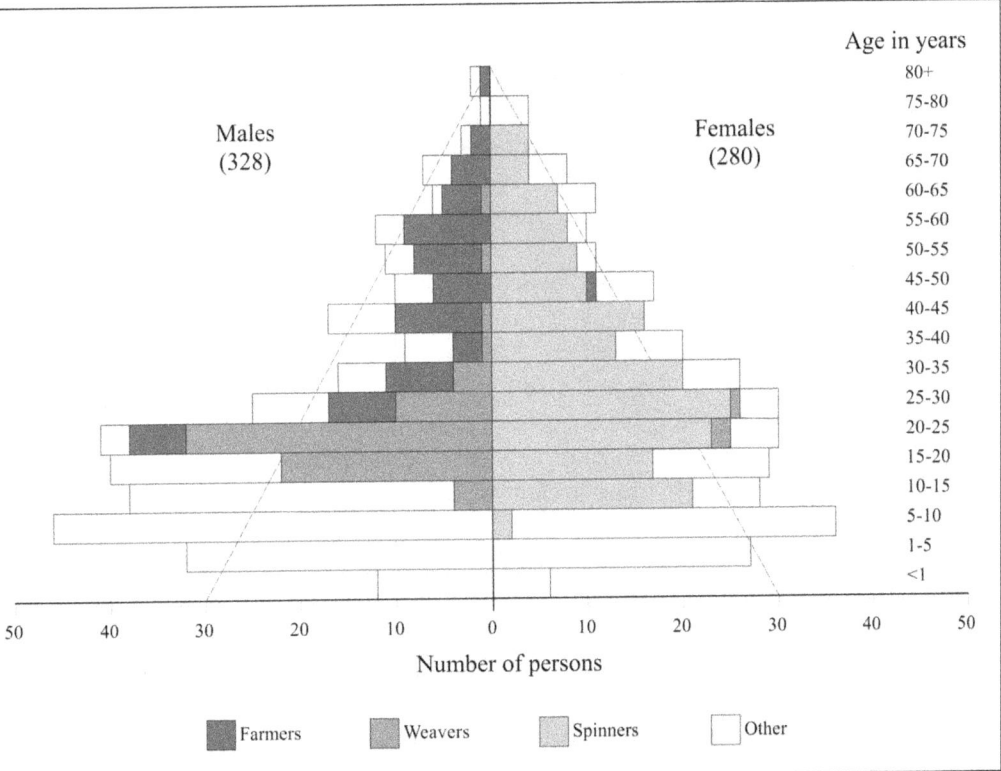

Fig. 1.1: Population structure of Derryhale townland, 1821

Figure 1.1 demonstrates that the townland had a relatively well-balanced demographic profile and that several of its residents survived beyond seventy years of age. However, there is some evidence, that girls and young women in the age group of ten to twenty-five years may have been leaving the townland in greater numbers than their male counterparts: possibly migrating as domestic servants and spinners to other places in Ulster or abroad. Interestingly, Wilson's wife, Jemima, would have fitted into this category when she emigrated to Canada in her early teens.

For young and old alike local employment had a rhythmic character forged by symmetry of the seasonal requirements of agriculture and the ubiquitous household presence of spinning wheels and linen looms. Occupations and their descriptions were fluid: the balance between weaving and farming altered not only in the context of seasonal demands but also evolved as individuals matured and succeeded to a leasehold interest in a piece of land, thereby acquiring the description of farmer. The physically demanding task of operating linen handlooms was the preserve of men and there were ninety such operatives, predominantly aged 15 to 30 years, living in the townland in 1821. However, few farmers older than thirty would have lacked the skill to weave and they probably resorted to it during late autumn and winter months.

It was a community in which childhood and adolescence were attenuated by the need to contribute to the family income by early employment. Within the dense rural settlement of Derryhale many children were recorded as having specific occupations and, almost certainly, many more would have been called upon for occasional assistance with farming, household, and linen manufacturing tasks. Girls as young as nine were returned as spinners, boys in their mid-teens were apprenticed to linen weavers, and others of a similar age were defined as servant boys and girls. Childhood was not a prolonged period of play and schooling: children were important economic assets in an intensive and delicately balanced economy.[7] For example, all of the 247 females older than ten years of age were recorded as having a defined occupation and the overwhelming majority of them (189) were engaged in spinning linen yarn. In an age spectrum ranging from ten to seventy years, girls, wives and widows were vital elements in supporting a community constructed around complex family economies.

When Wilson's father was forced off his farm c. 1832, he forfeited a critical augmentation of his income as a weaver and his rapid descent into poverty is comprehensible. His social descent was all the more inevitable as it would appear that he had no daughters or other sons living with him to supplement the family income through spinning and weaving. In such constrained circumstances the hiring out of Wilson at twelve years of age is entirely understandable. The 1821 census identified sixteen persons described as servant boys and servant girls in Derryhale: their ages ranged from nine years and upwards and the hiring of Wilson was not in any way anomalous.

The Cullen household was listed in the 1821 census as containing William and his wife, Mary and their five children. Only the two youngest, Robert and Mary, were not assigned an occupation and the engagement of the remainder of the family with the domestic linen industry was striking:

> Wm. Cullen, aged 40, farmer, 3 acres
> Mary Cullen, wife, aged 40, flax spinner
> Frances Cullen, son, aged 17, linen weaver
> Ann Cullen, dauter, aged 14, flax spinner
> Wm. Cullen, son, aged 12, linen weaver
> Robt. Cullen, aged 10
> Mary Cullen, dauter, aged 7, at school

The age structure and occupational characteristics of the Cullen family were typical of the region in 1821 and by the time Benson was hired in 1833 many of the sons and daughters of that household may have been no longer living with their parents, creating scope for hired household labour. At the termination of that employment Benson was again hired out to another local man, William Hyde, a reed maker where his income was increased by fifty percent to "6s. 6d. per quarter".[8] The William Hyde in question most probably lived in the adjacent townland of Bottlehill. The post-famine Griffith land valuation records indicate that a Hyde family lived in that townland, next door to William Courtney, the weaver with whom Wilson was later to serve an extensive apprenticeship.[9]

Benson claimed that he remained with Hyde for three years but his duties were not specified. If he served his time as an apprentice reed maker, learning a specialized skill, he did not deem it worthy of mention. More likely he was hired to perform general domestic duties, assisting in a rudimentary and occasional manner with the manufacture of reeds for the local linen looms. After his employment with Hyde, Wilson returned to his father's house for a few months, during which time he attended a day-school where he managed to receive "a few months schooling, being nearly all the day-schooling I ever attended". Later he was to supplement this education by attendance at Sunday school. Fortunately for him, that part of north Co. Armagh had a good network of privately supported schools that anticipated the National School system, then being established. Mullentine townland where his father now lived contained, according to the Ordnance Survey memoirs of 1835–8, "a school under Lord

7

Mandeville's superintendence".[10] This sojourn with his father likely occurred during winter months allowing him to avail of the opportunity offered by the local school. Some time later he continued his life as a hired labourer by moving temporarily to Scotland in the company of his sister who had emigrated there some time previously. He took with him 12s 6d, a sum equivalent to six month's remuneration from his period as a servant with Hyde.

The Scottish Experience

On a clear day the hills of Galloway in southwest Scotland, some thirty kilometres distant, are visible from the coastlines of Antrim and Down. Over many centuries, and in several different formats, migration streams and trade have bonded communities on either side of the relatively narrow North Channel. Permanent and seasonal migrations, educational and marriage links, as well as technological exchanges in shipbuilding, engineering and textile industries have all served to cement strong and active linkages between Scotland and Ulster. In general terms, migrants from Ulster traditionally favoured Scotland and northwest England as destinations of opportunity; migrants from other parts of Ireland tended to avail of shipping links with England.

By the 1820s steamships, mostly paddle-wheelers, had begun to service routes linking Derry, Larne and Belfast with the southwest Scottish ports of Portpatrick and Stranraer, as well as Glasgow and Greenock on the Clyde. The new mode of transport, reduced the duration of the voyage and greatly increased passenger capacity but for several more years fishing boats and small cargo vessels continued to ply their ways between a myriad of smaller ports in Ulster and Scotland. Irrespective of type, the boats crossing to Scotland were crammed to capacity and neither comfort nor safety were given much consideration.[11] When Benson sailed to Scotland he went from the Co. Down port of Donaghadee on a small sailing boat, arriving in Portpatrick "drenched with spray and rain". On his return trip some six months later, regardless of his temporary impoverishment, he "embarked on board the steamer *Arab,* for Belfast". Disembarking in Belfast, the adventurous Benson paid six pence for a trip by train to Lisburn and then walked the remainder of the journey to Co. Armagh – "a distance of twenty three Irish miles."[12] His identification of these two modes of transport for his return journey provide markers that allow us to date his trip with more precision than that suggested by his own narrative which is distorted by the vagaries of memory and singularly devoid of precise dates in this section. On a first reading it would appear that his sojourn in Scotland refers to 1836 when he was fifteen years of age. A closer reading of the text suggests that his Scottish experience was most likely to have occurred three years later. Historical records indicate that the *Arab*, a paddle steamer, was built in Glasgow in 1835 and it served the Glasgow, Belfast and Dublin routes on a regular basis for twenty years before being scrapped in 1855.[13] However, his reference to taking a train for the Belfast to Lisburn portion of his journey places the journey at least three years later. The railway line between Belfast and Lisburn carried its first train on August 12, 1839 and it is most likely that he travelled that route later that year.

Benson would, therefore, have been about eighteen years old when he arrived at Portpatrick, in the company of his sister and brother-in-law, to seek employment. They would not have been alone: by the second quarter of the nineteenth century thousands of men and a lesser number of women travelled annually from Ulster to Scotland in search of seasonal employment. The migratory labourers generally originated in the poorer agricultural regions of west and south Ulster and their seasonal earnings were a vital supplement to their otherwise meagre incomes and limited food resources. In Co. Armagh, half of the migrants originated in the poorer uplands of the south of the county but, in a striking extension of this geographical pattern, the more northerly Kilmore parish, home of the Benson family, was also recognised as an important source region of migrants.[14] The natural agricultural resources of Kilmore parish were undoubtedly superior to those of the Fews Mountains thirty kilometres to the south but Kilmore's exceptionally high population density of more than 130 persons per square kilometre compelled many residents to seek temporary employment elsewhere. Benson's foray into Scotland was, therefore, remarkably typical of his home community. The familiarity of the tradition of seasonal migration, together with the company of his older sister and brother-in-law, would have given him confidence and support for his first trip abroad. In the novel landscape and settlements of Scotland he would find additional support from fellow Ulstermen. By 1839 the legacy of the strong flow of Ulster migrants to the rapidly industrializing centres of the Scottish lowlands had created Irish enclaves, frequently segregated on a religious basis, in virtually every town and city. The census of 1841 recorded 126,321 Irish-born persons, equivalent to five percent of the population, residing permanently in Scotland. Almost one-third of them were living in Glasgow. For the young Benson there was a perceptible familiarity in the Scottish environment and he proved himself adept in availing of the support networks that it offered.

In international terms, the Scotland in which Benson arrived was urbanizing at a rate second only to that of England and Wales, and at a rate considerably more rapid than Ireland's. It has been estimated that almost thirty percent of Scots lived in towns of 10,000 or more by 1850; the equivalent figure for Ireland was only ten percent. The scale and rate of Scottish urbanization and associated opportunities for employment drew thousands of Scots from the rural lowlands and created scope for Irish and other seasonal migrants to fill the consequent void in the labour pool for agriculture. Thousands more Irish settled permanently in the industrial centres. Four of the five fastest growing towns in Scotland in the early nineteenth century were located in the Clyde basin, where the tobacco and sugar trades, textile manufacturing, and engineering works underpinned remarkable urban growth and development.

During these same years when the Irish were flooding into Scotland, native Scots were emigrating to England and across the Atlantic in ever-increasing numbers. This migration created a concomitant influx and exodus that has been described as "the Scottish paradox".[15] It was a period of considerable demographic flux for in addition to the long-term and permanent migrations a distinctive short term, or seasonal migration, to take up harvest employment flowed eastwards across Scotland in a zone stretching from Ayreshire in the west to the Lothians in the east. Planting, hay making, grain harvesting and potato picking created an extended season of opportunity from April to October and the scale of Scottish farming, especially in the east, required thousands of harvesters who travelled in groups across the country, availing of rudimentary temporary accommodation as they went. Usually organised under a single leader, work gangs from both the Scottish highlands and Ireland were commonplace in Ayrshire, the Clydeside industrial centres, and in the harvest fields of rich farmlands east of Edinburgh. It was a significant population movement of mostly young workers and friction and fights were not uncommon between, and within, the migrant groups.

Almost 20,000 seasonal migrants from Ulster travelled to Britain in 1841, the majority of them to Scotland.[16] By 1851, notwithstanding a reduction in the number of seasonal migrants, it was reported that 12,000 Irish reapers accompanied by at least 1,000 women and children were employed as seasonal workers in the East Lothians alongside, seasonal migrants from the Scottish highlands.[17] The Scottish historian, Thomas Devine, has argued that "highland workers continued to play an important role in lowland agriculture until the final few decades of the nineteenth century"[18] and were only able to off-set the lower wage costs of the Irish by virtue of their filling a distinctive niche in the local labour market. Highlanders, Devine asserts, could compete effectively with the Irish migrants because the Highlanders composed of a majority of women filled a specialist role by their use of the saw-toothed sickle. The scythe-hook that was favoured by the Irish men required less bending but was less effective than the saw-toothed sickle in harvesting lodged or fallen stalks of grain. [19]

In general, however, Irish migrants had an advantage as they were known to be willing to undercut local wage rates and had an added attraction in that they appeared when required and, mostly, disappeared when the harvest was completed. A contemporary observer in Glasgow gave a further reason for the competitiveness of the Irish labour noting:

> The Highlanders are unable to compete with the Irish who are landed for 6d a head, or perhaps less, by the steamboats in the very heart of Scotland, and near the agricultural districts, whereas the poor Highlanders have a long inland journey to perform.[20]

Benson's sojourn in Scotland in the spring and summer of 1839 was perhaps more varied than that of many of his fellow travellers. He worked in a number of niche occupations, some of them lasting only a few days. At times he went off on his own; on other occasions he remained with his sister and brother-in-law in a larger group setting. None of his jobs required any great competency other than astuteness and self-confidence, but his experience demonstrates fluidity between industrial and agricultural employment that has generally not been recognized in migration studies. Benson embraced effortlessly an amalgam of urban and rural activities and he was to re-enact this fluid pattern many times during his early years in Canada.

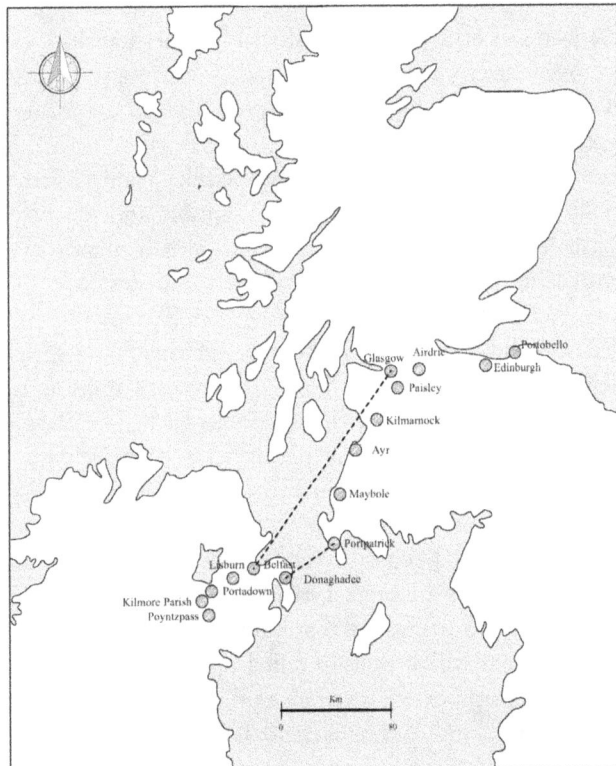

Fig. 1.2: Significant places in Wilson Benson's life, Ulster and Scotland

11

Commencing their Scottish adventure, Benson, his sister, and brother-in-law made their way through Ayrshire, staying "two days in the town of Ayr with a relative" before eventually arriving in the vibrant city of Glasgow where his brother-in-law quickly got work as a weaver and Benson found employment in a textile mill. Their accommodation needs were met by renting a house from James Smith who had come to Glasgow from Co. Derry some time previous. The call of open spaces intervened, however, and young Benson soon quit the factory job to set off on his own, peddling goods not only in Glasgow itself but also in the neighbouring towns of Paisley, Ruglin, Breg and Busby. At that time the appearance of itinerant Irish peddlers was a common sight in both Scotland and England where a contemporary report noted:

> [The Irish] fill all the low departments of retail dealing, as itinerant hawkers and peddlers or vendors of fruit and other provisions, many of them likewise keep spirit shops of various degrees of respectability. [In Kilmarnock] a great number of Irish hawkers are constantly in the town, dealing in drapery goods, braces, currycombs, spectacles, brass candlesticks, and small articles of hardware of every description.[21]

Benson was obviously successful in his salesmanship, earning eight shillings per week over a five-month period. It was many multiples of his income as a servant in rural Ulster. It served also as a prototype for his retailing activities in Canada.

In support of his efforts as a peddler tramping the roads of southern Scotland Benson drew upon the support and perceived familiarity of the Irish community in Glasgow. Eighteen pence worth of credit for miscellaneous goods was extended to him by "Mr. John White, a Belfast merchant, doing business below the Salt market, Glasgow." Although Benson did not identify the type of merchandise it likely consisted of relatively small portable items of hardware such as tinware, needles and nails that could be easily fitted into his pack. The 1836 post office directory for Glasgow confirms the presence of John Whyte, wholesale hardware merchant, at 90 Saltmarket Street, and a contemporary street directory for Belfast records the presence of John White, hardware merchant and ironmonger, 6 Bridge Street.[22] The mercantile linkage that connected family business in both Glasgow and Belfast was further proof of the numerous and strong ties that bound both cities, creating a familiar cultural environment which Benson relied upon for accommodation, and financial and moral support. His reliance on that community did not always have a positive outcome, however, and he was to discover that an Irish weaver,

Robert Young, with whom he lodged his earnings for safekeeping proved to be less than trustworthy; Young refused to return the money. Nevertheless, the buying and selling of goods provided valuable business experience for Benson. In later years in Canada he resorted to peddling and selling whiskey and ultimately established a general store in Markdale when he was no longer physically capable of continuing to operate his frontier farm.

Towards the end of the summer of 1839 Benson and his brother-in-law left Glasgow for the harvest fields of the Lothians some forty miles distant. En route they encountered several other harvest workers. His descriptions of ensuing fights, subterfuges used to obtain food while travelling, and their use of threats of disease to obtain assistance provide good insight into the group culture of the migrant harvesters. Locals viewed the newcomers with degrees of fear and suspicion. The fact that many of the Ulster migrants were drawn from Catholic communities on the southern and western peripheries of the province contributed further animus for distrust. A mid-nineteenth-century Edinburgh newspaper stridently proclaimed the basis for such distrust. It editorialised "We deeply lament and condemn the introduction into counties like East Lothian sets of low Popish Irish that bring with them their debasing habits, their turbulence, their blind superstitions ..."[23]

Benson would not have incurred the brunt of religious bigotry for he was Protestant by birth and upbringing but he was extremely conscious of the extent of the social and religious differences projected by the bands of Irish and Scottish migrants trudging through small Scottish communities to the rich grain farmers in the alluvial plains of Fifeshire. "Fights between the two branches of the Celtic family were of daily occurrence", he noted, and serious injury or death often resulted from the fracas.[24] Competition for scarce resources and labour opportunities in circumstances where migrants were usually organised into travelling groups under the leadership of a "ganger" provided the context for such inter-group affrays. In similar circumstances, soon after his arrival in Canada, Benson was to observe comparable tensions and strife emanating from within the context of transplanted immigrant rivalry.

On the way to the harvest fields Benson stopped in Edinburgh where he opportunistically "procured a small stock of fancy articles, which brought me some profit".[25] He conducted his resumed peddling activities in the vicinity of the resort town of Portobello and after a brief period he transferred into the employ of a local grain farmer named Hope. His assigned duties for the next three weeks consisted of assisting "a boy and a girl making porridge for some three hundred hands employed in the harvest".[26] The fact that Benson was employed in food preparation instead of working in the grain fields would suggest that his physique was not up to the demands of hard manual work and, in any event, there was nothing in his Co. Armagh experiences that would have taught him how to use a sickle in a manner to compete effectively with older, and more skilled, harvesters.

His employer was probably William Hope of Duddington Farm, Portobello, a prominent agriculturalist in the region where farms were large in scale and progressively managed.[27] Benson was charged with helping to feed three hundred workers who had been engaged to harvest "upwards of one thousand acres of land in various kinds of grain".[28] It has been estimated that six men with sickles could harvest an acre of grain per day and the implied output of Benson's three hundred fellow shearers would therefore have been fifty acres per day, or almost one thousand acres in the three weeks period spent on that farm.[29] Young Benson was an astute observer and recorder of the nature of the novel operation in which he was working. The scale of the Hope farm, and the associated workforce, portrayed an agricultural system than had no equivalent in Ireland. It was alien to his sense of miniscule holdings and subsistence farming in Co. Armagh. Even by the standards that Benson was to encounter some years later in Canada, the Hope farm was exceptionally large. Not until the opening up of the American mid-west for commercial grain farming in the mid-nineteenth century, and the subsequent extension of that system into the Canadian prairies, was such a scale of arable farming replicated in the New World. By then the technology of the horse-drawn reaper, binder and the combine harvester sustained a scale of agricultural production and a land-labour ratio that would have been inconceivable in an era of sickles and scythes.

At the conclusion of the harvest Benson returned via Glasgow to Belfast and onwards to his home district in Co. Armagh. He chose the paddle-steamer *Arab* for his conveyance. Unfortunately, having been defrauded by his Glasgow friend, Young, his total surviving accumulated earnings amounted to no more than one shilling, half of which he spent on the train fare from Belfast to Lisburn, availing of the recently completed railway line that linked the two places. Six months in Scotland had broadened his experience of life, extending confidence in his ability to tackle a variety of unskilled jobs but it had not provided any stability or development in his personal wealth. He was more impoverished than he had been when he set out from Donaghadee port in the springtime.

Final Months in Ireland

Returning to Co. Armagh in the autumn of 1839, Benson spent the next year much as he had done in the period immediately before embarking on his Scottish adventure. Within days he re-entered the wage economy, signing on for six months with his old employer, the reed maker Hyde, and subsequently moving fifteen kilometres to work for James Ford in the

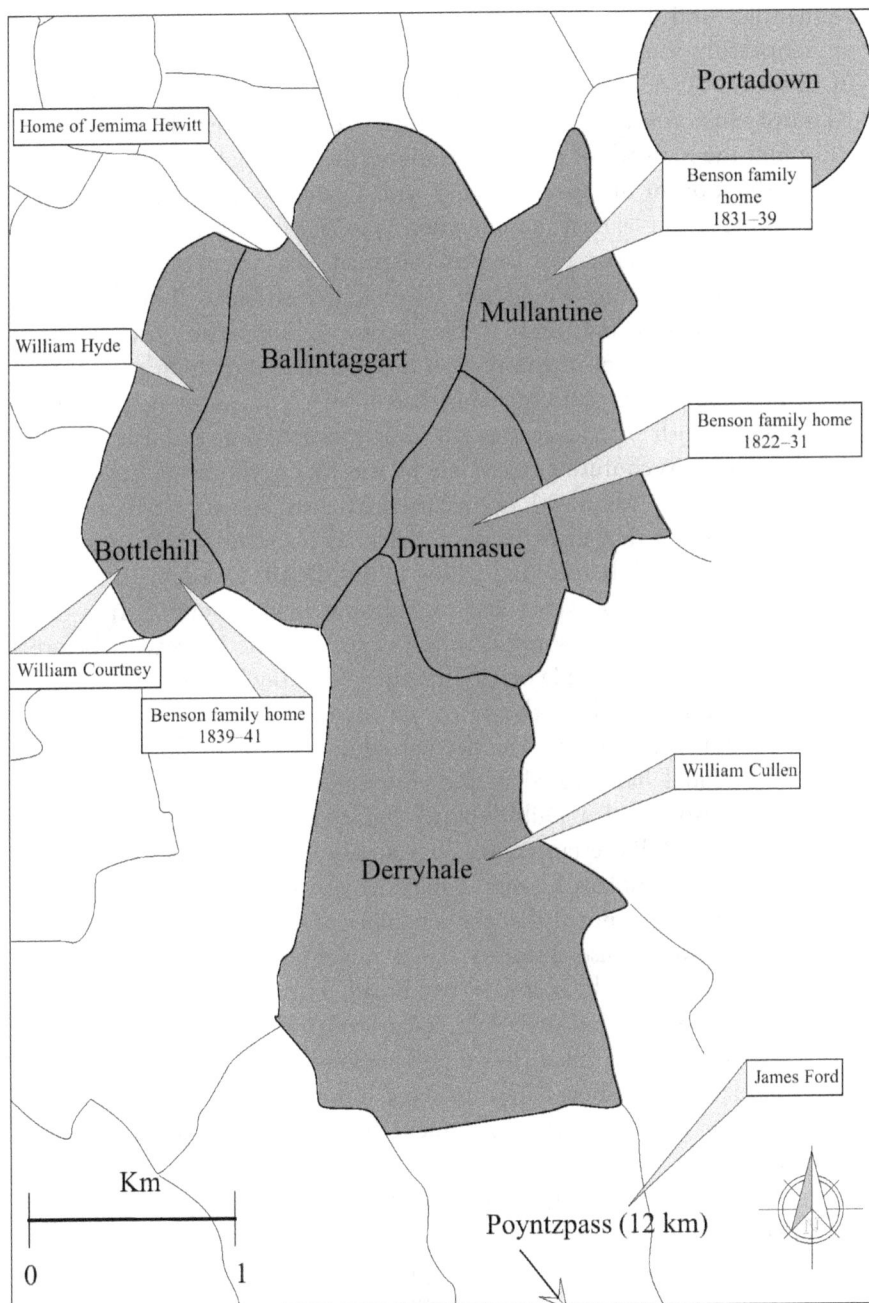

Home of Jemima Hewitt

Portadown

Benson family
home
1831–39

William Hyde

Mullantine

Ballintaggart

Benson family home
1822–31

Bottlehill

Drumnasue

William Courtney

Benson family home
1839–41

William Cullen

Derryhale

James Ford

Km

0   1

Poyntzpass (12 km)

Fig. 1.3: Wilson Benson's world, Kilmore parish, Co. Armagh

townland of Cruebeg, near the village of Poyntzpass. Ford was a farmer of some substance and Benson was probably employed once more as a general servant and labourer.[30] Benson then returned to his father's home in

Mullantine and having spent two months with him he entered an apprenticeship to a weaver, William Courtney, in the adjoining townland of Bottlehill. As demonstrated by Figure 1.3, the townlands of this part of Kilmore parish constituted a small and intimate world where distances were short and the network of personal relationships were highly localised. The agreed duration of his apprenticeship with Courtney was supposed to be four years and the agreed remuneration was "a guinea a year and a new shirt".[31] In his narrative Benson claimed that he completed the apprenticeship but this would not have been possible within the time period remaining to him prior to his documented departure for Canada. Either the vagaries of memory had exaggerated the duration of his apprenticeship or his apprenticeship had been commenced in the years before his Scottish experience. Benson's description of time and dates at this point in his life is confusing. Certainly he was living with his father on the night of the "Big Wind" which occurred in early January 1839 and he described how on that night of unprecedented storminess "The roof was taken off my father's house. And falling rafters, beams and debris smashed every thread in a linen web I had recently put in the loom".[32] It is this account that suggests Wilson had acquired an expertise in weaving before he left for Scotland a couple of months after "The Big Wind".

While residing with his father in the townland of Bottlehill, Benson had the opportunity to augment his formal education by attending Sunday school. A school had existed in the community since 1826. Operating under the auspices of a Dublin-based charity Bottlehill School had an enrolment of 80 Protestants and 20 Catholics in the mid-1830s. The headmaster was Absolam Hewitt, a member of the Church of Ireland. A contemporary report noted that the schoolhouse itself was a fine structure being "a neat stone house, 2 storeys, slated. It was built in 1826, not known what cost. It is 35 feet long and 17 feet broad. The upper part is occupied as a dwelling by the master".[33] Literacy levels in the local community probably would have been above the national average and the basic education received by Benson was to stand him in very good stead in later life, not only in his future employment but also in the writing of his autobiography.

In addition to improving his basic level of education Benson continued to perfect his skills as a weaver of fine linen cloth. He recounted, with some pride, the quality of the work that he produced for two linen drapers, Mr Dunbar of Banbridge and William Bennett of Tanderagee. The weaving of defined lengths of linen fabric, prescribed time for completion of the work, and payment calibrated to take account of the quality of the finished product were core elements of the new "putting out system" of the industry. Linen drapers and merchants were increasingly dominant: piecework was now common. Evolution of the linen industry into large-scale production in factories powered by coal-generated steam was already underway. The Mr Dunbar to whom Wilson referred was probably Hugh Dunbar (1789–1847) who was responsible in 1838 for the construction of the massive Dunbar, McMaster & Co. Ltd. spinning mill in the factory village of Gilford, a few kilometres distant from Banbridge. He had also built another factory in 1839 that was dedicated to the production of fine linen and cambric cloth in the nearby village of Tullylish.[34] By the time he was eighteen Wilson had been introduced to the transformative elements of modernity in the Ulster economy: steamboats, railways and factory production were all incorporated into his life experience along with a familiarity with a much older proto-industrial economy based on a complex union of small scale agriculture and domestic craft textile industry. He would bring the experience of both, together with a respect for change and progress, to his subsequent life in Canada. The decision to emigrate to Canada would not be taken alone. In 1839 he had:

> made the acquaintance of a young lady named Miss Jemima Hewitt, who attended the same Sabbath school as myself. She had learned the dressmaking profession in Rich Hill. Our acquaintance soon ripened into a closer relationship than friendship, and we were married privately, our extreme youth – I was eighteen years and she was sixteen years of age – rendering us doubtful if our respective parents would give consent to our union on that account. But on the fact becoming known to them, they one and all heartily acquiesced in our little ruse.[35]

Their marriage would appear to have taken place in the autumn of 1840 but Benson's description of the time frame of this pivotal event in his life is not entirely accurate, probably with good reason. The baptismal records of the Church of Ireland in Kilmore parish indicate that Jemima was born in 1828 and at the time of her marriage she would have just reached her twelfth birthday.[36] Even by the standards of pre-famine Ireland, Jemima was unusually young to be married and this probably accounts for the ceremony being conducted privately. No record of it appears in the registry of the local church. It may also explain why, in the months following their marriage, the two spouses continued to live with their respective parents. It may well also have been a motivating factor in Benson's emigration to Canada in the company of his wife a few months later, not to mention a reason for the two of them passing as brother and sister when they first arrived overseas.

On the eve of his twentieth year Benson was relatively well prepared for the challenges and dangers of emigration. He was skilled as a weaver and understood the futility of remaining in that craft in the face of the advance of factory production and steam power. His own father, who had left the weaving trade of Belfast to eke out a difficult living in farming and handloom weaving, provided a salutary example of Benson's likely future. In making his way in both Scotland and Ulster Benson experienced his own share of difficulties and he learned also to discriminate between those he could trust and those he should avoid. In his activities as a peddler and as a handloom weaver he navigated the borders of urban and rural life, moving frequently in search of work. The move to Canada was a logical extension of his earlier experiences. A deep-seated desire to succeed infused him and in his wife, Jemima, he found a life partner whose dressmaking skills were to prove very marketable. Together they were determined to make a new life on their own, and under conditions where hard work and dedication could break the cycle of impending poverty.

Notes and References

1 W.J Smyth, "The Social and Economic Geography of Nineteenth Century Co. Armagh", PhD thesis, 1973, the National University of Ireland.

2 "1835 Report From H.M. Commissioners For Inquiry Into The Conditions of The Poorer Classes in Ireland", British Parliamentary Papers, 1835, xxxiv, 289.

3 The Tithe Applotment books for Seagoe parish, 1834, show Bensons living in the townlands of Lylo, Crossmecaghley, Drumgor and Drumlisnagrilly. The latter townland is about six kilometres distant from that of Drumnasue where Wilson's father settled in 1821. He may well have had a family relationship with this group.

4 Benson, *Life and Adventures*, 89.

5 Two William Cullens are identifiable in the Tithe Applotment records for Kilmore parish in 1833. One lived in the townland of Ballywilly, some five miles west of Drumnasue, and the other lived in Derryhale, adjacent to Drumnasue and in close proximity to the other townlands that were recorded as featuring in the lives of Wilson and his father – Mullantine, Bottlehill and Ballintaggart. The manuscript census records for Kilmore parish in 1821 also confirm the presence of a William Cullen in Derryhale.

6 David Herbison (1800–80), "Midnight Musings, or Thoughts from the Loom", (Belfast: 1848). This poem is reprinted in the collection edited by John Hewitt, *Rhyming Weavers and the Country Poets of Antrim and Down* (Belfast: Blackstaff Press, 1974), 122. The eminent Ulster poet, John Hewitt, was himself a native of Kilmore parish in Co. Armagh.

7 The nature of employment in the Derryhale community was probably not unlike that described by Peter Laslett for pre-industrial England. Peter Laslett, *The World We Have Lost* (New York: Charles Scribner and Sons, 1971).

8 A reed maker was an artisan who fabricated wooden or metal devices that, when inserted into the mechanism of the handloom, regulated the density of warp threads in the linen fabric under production. For a more detailed explanation see S.C. Lutton, "The Linen Trade in Co. Armagh Since the Turn of the Century" in *Journal of the Craigavon Historical Society*, vol. 2, no. 3, 1970.

9 Griffith's Valuation, 1864, Bottlehill, Kilmore parish, Co. Armagh.

10 Ordnance Survey Memoirs, Kilmore parish, Co. Armagh, 1834. The original manuscript of the memoirs is held by The Royal Irish Academy, Dublin.

11 James E. Handley, *The Irish in Modern Scotland* (Cork: Cork University Press, 1938), 165. Handley describes the voyage of one such ship – *The Thistle* which sailed from Derry to Greenock in 1849 with a total of 1,900 passengers crammed onto the deck.

12 The *Arab* was recorded in Lloyd's *Register of Ships*, 1836. It is identified also in D.B. McNeill, *Irish Passenger Steamship Services*, vol. 2 (Newton Abbot: David and Charles, 1971), 192.

13 Lloyd's *Register of Ships*, 1836 and 1856.

14 This pattern was noted in the 1835 British government inquiry into the condition of the poorer classes in Ireland (British Parliamentary Papers, 1835, xxxiv) and has been mapped in Anne O'Dowd, *Spalpeens and Tattie Hokers, History and Folklore of the Irish Migratory Agricultural Worker In Ireland and Britain* (Dublin: Irish Academic Press, 1991), 83.

15 T.M. Devine (ed.), *Scottish Emigration and Scottish Society – Proceedings of the Scottish Historical Studies Seminar*, University of Strathclyde 1990–91, (Edinburgh: John Donald Publishers Ltd., 1992), 1.

16 T.W. Freeman, *Pre-Famine Ireland* (Manchester: Manchester University Press, 1957), 43.

17 Handley, *The Irish*, 166

18 T.M. Devine, *Exploring the Scottish Past: Themes in the History of Scottish Society* (East Linton: Tuckwell Press, 1995), 143.

19 Ibid., 145.

20 British Parliamentary Papers, Poor Inquiry, Ireland, 1836, Appendix D, 103.

21 British Parliamentary Papers, Poor Inquiry, Ireland, 1836, Appendix C, 5.

22 Post Office Annual Directory, Glasgow, 1836 and Martin's Belfast Directory, 1839.

23 Handley, *The Irish*, 168.

24 Benson, 95.

25 Ibid.

26 Ibid.

27 The "Post Office Annual Directory, Edinburgh and Surrounding Towns, 1833–1834" lists William Hope as the occupant of Duddington Farm, Portobello. He is the only agriculturalist of that name listed for the district.

28 Benson, 95.

29 Handley, *The Irish*, 166.

30 James Forde of Cruebeg is recorded in the Lord Mandeville Papers as being a registered 40-shilling freeholder on the Mandeville estate almost two decades earlier in 1820. This status gave him the right to vote in elections as a property holder and is suggestive of a stable and prominent position within the local community. The Mandeville Papers are held by the Public Record Office of Northern Ireland.

31 Benson, 98.

32 Benson, 99. Wilson erroneously attributes the "Big Wind" to the "fall of 1838". The meteorological event actually occurred in January 1839 and is regarded as being an unusual storm of hurricane status. Tremendous damage was done to property throughout Ireland and it was recorded that fish were washed out of the sea and dumped seven miles inland along the western coastline. When the old age pension was introduced for Irish residents over seventy years of age in 1911 an acceptable supporting proof of age was deemed to be whether or not the recipient was alive at the time of the "Big Wind". The historic significance of the night was projected across the Atlantic also. For example, Professor Peter Toner of the University of New

Brunswick recalls that family lore identified the departure of his great grandfather from Co. Derry for New Brunswick as occurring in the aftermath of that memorable night. When Professor Toner checked the New Brunswick immigration records he discovered that the family lore tallied to within a few months.

33 Ordnance Survey Memoirs, Co. Armagh, Kilmore parish, 1834.

34 Kathleen Rankin, *The Linen Houses of The Bann Valley* (Belfast: Ulster Historical Foundation, 2007).

35 Benson, 100.

36 Kilmore parish records have been viewed by the authors in their original manuscript form in the church vestry and also in microfilm form in the Public Record Office of Northern Ireland. Jemima was born to John and Dorothea Hewitt of Ballintaggart, November 14th, 1828. No other person of that name was baptized in the church in the period covered by Wilson Benson's life in Ireland. Cross-linkage with the Tithe Applotment books for Kilmore parish in the mid-1830s indicate that Jemima's father was a farmer in the neighbouring townland of Ballintaggart.

2

Making the Transatlantic Connection

Recently married but still living at home with his father, Benson decided to "try America in the spring [of 1841]." At that time the Canadian colonies of Upper and Lower Canada, New Brunswick, Nova Scotia and Prince Edward Island were referred to as British North America in official documents. While most Ulster people would have been aware of the geographical, political and economic separation of the Canadian territories from the United States, the vernacular use of the term "America" denoted a generalised transatlantic destination. It was not specific in geopolitical terms. In Benson's home locality of east Ulster, Canada had been the preferred destination for several years. A combination of cheap fares, perceived opportunities for free land, and the influence of personal contacts supported by a well-established process of chain migration had all encouraged a northward shift of an Ulster migration stream that had previously favoured the eastern seaboard of colonial America.

In the three decades from 1815 to 1845 Irish emigrants to North America amounted to about one million and at least half of them travelled by way of Canada. Probably less than half of the Canadian arrivals settled long-term in the British colonies since the border with the United States was long and highly permeable. A contra-flow of emigrants did enter Canada from the south but its size was modest. By 1840, however, the geography of transatlantic migration had begun to alter once more. Diminishing opportunities to acquire a grant of land and the lack of significant urban centres in Canada increasingly deflected a majority of aspiring emigrants southwards to the port cities of the north-eastern United States. By the onset of the Famine in 1845 American ports had become more popular destinations than their Canadian counterparts. This primacy was extended further when, following the disastrous year of "black '47", legislative changes and higher landing taxes in Canada resulted in most Irish emigrants henceforth sailing directly to the seaport cities of the United States. Thereafter emigration from Ireland to Canada slowed to a trickle, and the British colonies never recovered their previous parity of attraction with their southern neighbour. But even within a diminished cohort of emigrants to Canada Ulster people continued to be over-represented – a regional bias that persisted well into the twentieth century.[1]

As a consequence of this oscillation in their migration history the Irish in Canada emerged with a uniquely nuanced identity within the nineteenth- and twentieth-century development of a global Irish diaspora. The Canadian Irish are predominantly pre-famine in origin, whereas Irish communities in the United States, Australia, New Zealand and South Africa are predominantly Famine and post-famine in their genesis.[2] Furthermore, most of the Irish who settled in Canada in the first half of the nineteenth century located themselves in rural and small town environments – a settlement pattern that was in marked contrast to that of the highly urbanized Irish in the port and industrial cities of the north-eastern United States. The Canadian Irish were distinguished further by the fact that a majority were Protestant – Ulster being proportionately the most important source region. From the early eighteenth century a culture of emigration had been especially prevalent in that northern Irish province and the pronounced outflow of Presbyterians to the settlement frontier of colonial America created communities to which the descriptor of Scotch-Irish was later applied.[3] Co. Armagh had been strongly represented among those early pioneers and that tradition was reinvigorated in the early nineteenth century with the return of maritime trade, especially in timber, and the availability of ships for emigrant travel following the conclusion of the Napoleonic wars.

In terms of its regional economic background, timing, and choice of destination the narrative of Benson conforms closely to this generalised pattern of pre-famine emigration. He was a Protestant from a linen weaving background in Co. Armagh and within his family and among his neighbours, weavers and farmers alike, there was an established tradition of emigration. In the years immediately preceding his departure thousands from the locality had opted to convert their assets into passages on the growing number of ships plying the Atlantic trade. Others sought employment in the growing industrial centres of Scotland and England and quite a few migrated the short distance to Belfast. The most destitute, generally landless labourers immobilised by poverty, remained in an Ireland that was moving inexorably towards demographic calamity. Even in Ulster, where much of the population had some access to non-agricultural supplementary incomes, a high number of famine deaths occurred.

Benson did not have personal access to land but he was a skilled craftsman, having served his apprenticeship as a handloom weaver, and for some time before his departure he had been a participant in a waged

22

economy. He was familiar with having to move his abode to obtain employment, either within the immediate locale of north Armagh or further afield to Scotland. Although the prospects of a long transatlantic voyage did engender some dread he and his wife were prepared for the challenge. Aggregate statistics for contemporary emigrants suggest that the largest component were young single adults, but there is evidence to support the contention that married couples and families represented at least a quarter of those who eventually settled in Canada.[4] The Bensons were not unique in any aspect of their demographic profile. Amongst those leaving Ireland, and among the tens of thousands of fellow countrymen who settled in towns and along the agricultural frontier of the Great Lakes Basin, they were indeed very typical.

In common with many of his fellow countrymen, Benson was well aware that those contemplating a transatlantic voyage were likely to experience hardship and possibly death from shipwreck, disease and drowning. A sustained flow of letters from earlier emigrants provided considerable details on the expected nature of the voyage, appropriate preparations for departure and advice on the best way of surviving the challenge of being cooped up on a small ship for several weeks in the company of hundreds of strangers. Wilson Benson was well aware that:

> Seven, eight, nine, and as high as thirteen weeks were not unfrequently occupied by sailing vessels on the voyage; and the consequent suffering experienced on such occasions, the news of which, when transmitted by the sufferers to relatives at home, had spread an universal dread of a trip to America.[5]

Whether by good fortune or an informed choice of ship, Wilson and Jemima escaped the worst horrors of the trip. To be sure, one fellow passenger did die but there would appear to have been an adequate supply of food and water on board. Notwithstanding Benson's description of the captain as being "partially insane", there is no doubt but that a skilled crew ensured the vessel's survival during a dangerous Atlantic storm and coped also when the ship was becalmed off the southern coast of Newfoundland. Benson's independent spirit reacted negatively to the officious behaviour of the captain and the stern treatment of both passengers and crew. This animosity, together with his tendency to be melodramatic, coloured his later recollections. However, it was mere fanciful thinking on his part that the ship "was lost on her return voyage, but the crew were saved, and the captain died of brain fever afterwards."[6] There is plenty of evidence that the ship remained in service long after its 1841 voyage. The *Sarah Stewart* was still sailing the Atlantic in 1846 although by that time she had switched from the Canadian route to that of Belfast–New Orleans.[7] Captain Low remained in charge of long-distance vessels for several more years.

The autobiography does not provide a precise timetable for the duration of the voyage and indeed his overall account of the timing of the journey diverges slightly from ascertainable facts. According to *The Belfast Newsletter*, the *Sarah Stewart* left Belfast on April 5, not on March 28, as Wilson claimed. A storm "experienced on the 3rd and 4th of April" and a subsequent encounter with a stricken vessel must have occurred at least a week later.[8] He refers to viewing the Quebec landscape along the St Lawrence River "in the effulgent rays of an April sun"[9] but his sense of time was distorted, either by the mindless endurance of a tedious voyage or by the tricks of memory when he wrote his autobiography thirty-five years later. His journey up the St Lawrence took place in the middle of May and on May 22 his ship docked in Quebec City. The voyage had lasted forty-seven days.[10] Official guidelines for the duration of voyages to Quebec suggested forty-six days as an average. Emigration commissioners recommended in their published advice that the best period to arrive was "early in May, so as to be in time to take advantage of the Spring and Summer work, and to get settled before the Winter sets in."[11] In those respects Wilson Benson commenced his new life in Canada in good circumstances.

As testimony to the efficiency of news transmission in that period it is to be noted that the departure of the *Sarah Stewart* from Belfast was reported in *The Belfast Newsletter* in its coverage of local port and shipping news on April 9 – "The barque Sarah Stewart of Belfast, Captain Low, sailed hence, on Monday, for Quebec with 273 passengers." In Canada *The Quebec Mercury* gave early notice of the ship's expected arrival on May 11 (advance information having been brought via a fast mail-ship) and its actual arrival was published two weeks later by the same Quebec paper. Communications in that pre-famine era were more efficient than is sometimes realised and played a significant role in the emigration economy. Public and private communication bridged the Atlantic with efficiency, inculcating the idea of emigration into the mindset of individuals and diverse communities in Ireland and maintaining for perspective emigrants an awareness of how to proceed.

The *Sarah Stewart* was only one of many ships that departed Belfast for Canada that spring: most sailed by way of the principal route to Quebec City with several other vessels sailing to St John, New Brunswick.[12] Indeed, a total of sixteen ships carrying 4,412 passengers to Quebec City departed Belfast in 1841 and seven of them, including that carrying Wilson and Jemima, were under charter to the merchant firm of G.H. Parke and Co. who maintained offices in both Belfast and Quebec. Carrying a total of 2,618 individuals this mercantile firm was responsible for sixty percent of the emigrant trade out of Belfast that year and was unquestionably the largest operator in the field. In addition to their human cargo, three of their ships carried manufactured goods and salt, the latter probably originating in either Cheshire or in the salt deposits of nearby Carrickfergus. Two ships under charter to other companies transported rigging and cordage, the product of Belfast's rope works, but in general the relatively small Canadian population generated only a limited demand for the outputs of the British industrial revolution and that market potential was further limited by strong competition from goods manufactured in the United States.

All ships departing for Canada carried considerable tonnage of ballast as a stabilizer on the long Atlantic voyage and Canadian quaysides still retain thousands of tons of Irish rock and debris transported for weight not monetary value.[13] A much higher cargo value for these ships would be realized on the eastward voyage when the temporary bunks for steerage passengers, were removed to accommodate timber, wheat and flour destined for British and Irish ports.[14] The products of the rich stands of virgin forest in New Brunswick, Ontario, and Quebec provided essential material for the house and factory construction booms of industrializing Britain. To the present day many buildings in Belfast and elsewhere in Ireland contain structural elements made from Canadian timber.

Destination Quebec

The centrality of Quebec City to the Irish emigrant trade was a direct outcome of the geographical realities governing access to the North American continent. Quebec City was much more than a destination: it was the gateway not only to Canada but also to upper New York State, the Great Lakes Basin, the Ohio River Valley, and the Midwest interior. St John, New Brunswick, provided access to the limited agricultural potential of New Brunswick and Nova Scotia and acted also as a conduit for emigrants heading south to New England, New York City, and other cities on the eastern seaboard. American ports such as Boston, New York City and Philadelphia were also popular among Irish immigrants and, given the scale and complexity of their urban development, they were primary destinations in themselves as well.

Emigrants seeking passage to Canada in 1841 had several commercial options in Ireland to choose from and the ultimate decision was probably determined by proximity to a port, advice from relatives and the directive influences of pre-paid tickets and the local network of agents. There is little evidence that the cost of passage varied significantly between the departure ports; emigrants could expect to pay in the region of £3 10s. per person, slightly more if the ship had a generous stock of provisions. Sixteen Irish ports and ninety-eight ships conveyed 16,173 passengers directly to Quebec in 1841 and of those Belfast was undoubtedly the most important, with Limerick occupying second place. The number of emigrants arriving from the Irish ports is presented here in Table 2.1.

Table 2.1

PORTS OF ORIGIN OF IRISH IMMIGRANTS LANDING IN QUEBEC IN 1841

Port	Passengers	No. Ships	Port	Passengers	No. Ships
Belfast	4,412	16	Newry	540	3
Limerick	2,229	17	Tralee	510	2
Derry	1,766	8	New Ross	505	2
Cork	1,453	10	Westport	148	1
Dublin	1,257	9	Galway	122	2
Sligo	1,223	9	Youghal	104	3
Waterford	733	7	Wexford	45	1
Killala	572	4			
Donegal	554	4	Total	16,173	98

A quarter of the emigrants had made the same choice as Benson, selecting Belfast which, along with Newry, served east Ulster. More than half of the emigrants depicted in Table 2.1 departed through Ulster ports and the adjoining port of Sligo. The scale difference between the traffic departing from Belfast and Derry reflects the fact that the latter port sent most of its emigrants to New Brunswick in that year while Belfast, mainly but not exclusively, served Quebec. The number of emigrants landing in the Atlantic provinces of New Brunswick, Nova Scotia and Prince Edward Island amounted to about half of those travelling via the St Lawrence to the gateway port of Quebec City. The number of Irish arriving in New Brunswick in 1841 has been established as 7,291.[15] The official contemporary estimate for the total number of Irish disembarking in all the Canadian colonies in 1841 tallied some 24,000 individuals but some scholars have argued that this figure omits those Irish who sailed via Liverpool and Greenock. Numbers were further distorted by the counting of children as fractions of adult passengers.[16] By way of correction some authors have posited a total of 30,000 arrivals: reliance on either figure confirms that emigration from Ireland to Canada had assumed the dimension of a flood of mass migration. At least half of the emigrants had originated in Ulster where consideration of transatlantic opportunities was part of the life choices contemplated by a majority of families.[17]

Among the thousands of emigrants leaving Ireland in 1841 the Bensons were indeed fortunate in their local arrangements for the journey. Individuals and families emigrating from remoter areas in southwest Ulster faced tedious journeys to the seaports of Derry and Belfast. By carriage, horse and cart, and often on foot they made their way, over several days to the quayside boarding houses where they awaited notice to board. All of this represented additional cost as well as hardship. On the other hand the Bensons lived less than fifty kilometres from Belfast. No mention is made of their journey to the port city but it is likely that they travelled by horse and carriage as far as Lisburn and there boarded the train to Belfast.[18] Neither does Benson have anything to say about their wait in Belfast for the sailing to be announced. It is possible that they were permitted to board the *Sarah Stewart* on the date given by him (March 28) but that the ship did not leave Belfast harbour until a week later. Early boarding was at the discretion of the captain and delays in sailing often arose as ship owners delayed departure in the hope of picking up a few extra passengers. The autobiography is silent on the Belfast section of the journey; details are reserved for the adventures of the voyage itself.

Along with the other passengers aboard the *Sarah Stewart*, Wilson and his young wife were determined to "achieve a home and independence in the Western World which the force of circumstances denied me in the land of my birth."[19] Wilson had witnessed emigration from within his own family some years earlier when his sister moved to Scotland and Jemima, had one, and possibly two, brothers living in Canada. Many other neighbours and friends would have preceded his own emigration and consequently preparations for the trip incorporated what had become a familiar ritual in the locality: "leave-taking – messages from friends in Ireland to friends in Canada".[20] The exchange of transatlantic news, which Wilson Benson facilitated, was a regular and effective feature of emigrant life: it allowed families to keep in touch over several years as well as providing useful advice on conditions to be expected during travel and subsequently upon arrival. It was all part of a vibrant culture of emigration and it helped foster linkages not only with relatives remaining in Ireland but also facilitated connections between fellow immigrants in Canada, reducing the loneliness of the adventure and providing opportunity for practical advice on the settlement process.

Relatives and friends sent letters back from North America and the coveted news was read around kitchen tables and related in churches, lodge halls and marketplaces. Testimony from trusted people about the pitfalls likely to be encountered in the settlement process, identification of people and places to avoid, and the provision of the addresses of friends to call upon were highly valued. Given the long and vibrant tradition of emigration from Ireland and the regionally specific dimension of much of the outflow, it was scarcely surprising that most emigrants were already potential members of far-flung communities. The vibrancy of such communities and their relevance to the Bensons may be gauged from a letter from a fellow Ulsterman, James Humphrey of Moneymore, Co. Derry, who had landed in Quebec City in the spring of 1824 with his brother and sister and their respective families. Their route from Quebec City westward to Niagara (Fort George) and York (Toronto) was not dissimilar to that undertaken fifteen years later by Wilson and his wife. In a letter home Humphrey recounted the number of relatives, friends and former neighbours encountered along the way:

> We stopped two days in Quebec. It had a black appearance. There are full fine stores in it. I saw John Egnew, he was very kind to us. I saw James McCana, he is very well and is going home. He and Edward McAnaway, they were very kind to us. We then took a steamboat to Montreal and stayed two days there. Mr. Richardson went to Benjamin Workman and left the letter for Robert Workman. He told us he was there about two weeks ago and that he would be back in about eight days and they were well and doing well. We went and hired a wagon and went out nine miles to Lachine and there took a steamboat one hundred and fifty miles to Prescott. The first I saw was my sister Mary and she took us to her house and we stayed all night in her house and then we took the steamboat sixty miles to Kingston and we stopped there six days. You may let James Baylen know that I went out and saw George and he is well and he told us he would send his mother six pounds. Kingston is a good town and is very rich. Mr. Twig lives five miles out of town and William and I were out and he has a beautiful place. You may let Mrs. Johnston know that her brother Will Cranis is well and has a full fine shop. We went and got a steamboat and sailed to Fort George and found John and Robert Gilmore there and they are all in good health when I saw them … John Humphrey's Joseph is dead, he lived but two days after he landed at Fort George. The steamboat stopped about eight hours and then we went away to York. We landed on the 25th of August and went to John Richardson's place. He has 200 acres of good land and a house on it about two perches from the road. Two days after Margaret had a young daughter and it lived three weeks and I called it for my mother. I took a house three miles from their place and set up a tavern.[21]

It was an impressive listing and would have been reasonably representative of the social encounters to be expected on landing in the British North American colonies.

The community support provided by prior migrants was frequently augmented by financial aid in the form of remittances and pre-paid passages. An 1843 Belfast advertisement for passage on board the *Sarah Stewart* once more sailing from Belfast to Quebec City advised intending passengers:[22]

Those who hold orders or drafts on RYAN (Brothers) of
Quebec, or RYAN, CHAPMAN & CO., Montreal, will please
have their names forwarded immediately to the
subscriber, who will secure berths for them in the
Sarah Stewart, to sail on or about 10th April, from
Belfast for Quebec.
For terms of Passage, which are very moderate, apply
to
SAMUEL M'CREA
General Emigration Office, 37, Waring-street;
Or
to JAMES JOHNSTON, Augher.
Belfast, February 21, 1843.

The firms of Ryan (Quebec City) and Ryan, Chapman & Co.
(Montreal) referenced in the advertisement were important Irish links in
the contemporary emigration process.[23] Natives of Ballinakill, Co. Laois,
the Ryan brothers had settled in Quebec in the 1820s where they soon
developed a strong shipping business. They acted as agents for both Baring
and Lloyds of London. Thomas, the elder brother, later emerged as a
leading political and business leader among Montreal's Catholic Irish
community. Their advertised facility of pre-paid passages allowed Canadian
residents to lodge money in Quebec City or Montreal on behalf of Irish
relatives or friends preparing to emigrate, and in the process greatly
facilitated population mobility in pre-famine Ireland. Upwards of one third
of emigrants at the time were supported by pre-paid passages and
remittance money forwarded by relatives who had gone out earlier.[24]

There is no evidence that Benson availed of a pre-paid passage,
notwithstanding the fact that Jemima had siblings already settled in
Canada. As a skilled weaver he probably financed his journey by recourse
to earnings and savings. However, his wealth would have been modest and
when he arrived at the Grosse Isle quarantine station he had only two
sovereigns remaining in his pocket.[25] As a skilled artisan he would not have
been among the most destitute of his fellow passengers. In general terms he
conformed to the description that Belfast ships sailing to Quebec were
noted for conveying a superior class of passenger.[26] Indeed Benson's
assertion, in one instance, that fellow passengers raised a sum of five
hundred sovereigns, offering it to the captain as an incentive to return to
the homeport during a violent storm, confirms the presence of considerable
money among his fellow shipmates.

In preparation for the voyage, emigrants assembled as much money as
possible. In the case of tenant farming families in Ulster this often involved
the selling of improvements made to the house and lands being vacated.

Additional food supplies were often brought on board, along with luggage chests filled with clothes, personal effects, tools and small implements. Sometimes grass seeds from the home farm and favourite flower seeds were carried, and they would be planted both as a contribution to the seeding of cleared land and also as tangible mementoes of home.[27] Passengers travelling in cabin class had more capacity to bring items of furniture with them and, for example, the Fallona family, originally from Ballytrustan in Co. Down, has long treasured a fine oak table brought to North America aboard an emigrant ship in 1831.[28] Wilson Benson's luggage was of a more modest nature. His chest contained items of clothing for his wife and himself as well as bedclothes and he had the misfortune to have most of those possessions stolen shortly after disembarkation.

The *Sarah Stewart* was a 320-ton barque, built in Nova Scotia in 1838. Constructed of timber it was reinforced with iron bolts and would have been very typical of contemporary sailing vessels, combining trade in timber with the transportation of emigrants.[29] It was estimated that Canadian-built ships at that time sold in Britain for about £8 10s. per ton. Fit-out costs would have been additional.[30] As such it represented a considerable investment for the owners but a third of the construction cost would have been recouped by a single voyage containing 273 passengers each paying £3 10s. Canadian-built ships, generally built of softwood were regarded as being inferior to British-built vessels and their life expectancy was presumed to be little more than a decade.[31] The *Sarah Stewart* was only three years old at the time of Benson's voyage and it should have been in good repair. The ship was most likely a three- or four-mast vessel and, like other barques of its class it would have been both fast and easily managed. The vessel operated out of Belfast where its registered owner was J. Low.[32] The captain was listed as A. Low, presumably a family member, and like most ships at the time it was available for charter by interested mercantile firms. In this case it was chartered by G.H. Parke and Co. With an unladened weight of 320 tons the vessel should have taken on board no more than the equivalent of 190 passengers as the British shipping Act of 1835 stipulated that the number of passengers should not be greater than three for every five tons.[33] However, children were counted either as half an adult or not at all and consequently there was considerable discrepancy between the number of bodies on board and the permitted limit. With a total of 273 passengers, as recorded in *The Belfast Newsletter*, there is no doubt but that the ship was filled to capacity, or beyond.

Two years later, in the spring of 1843, another sailing of the *Sarah Stewart* from Belfast to Quebec City, again under the captaincy of Archibald Low, was preceded by a detailed advertisement and the attendant description on that occasion provides considerable ancillary detail about the physical dimensions of the vessel. Height between decks was advertised as being upwards of seven feet, a provision that was considerably in excess of the minimum of five and a half feet prescribed in the 1828 Passenger Act.[34] Additionally, the ship was described as having:

> a well-furnished Medicine Chest put on board for the use and comfort of her Passengers, together with an abundant supply of good Water and Fuel, which will render her a most desirable conveyance for Cabin, second Cabin, and Steerage Passengers ... Scale of Provisions and Water that will be provided to each Adult by the Ship during the voyage: – 7lbs. of Bread, Biscuit, Flour, Oatmeal, or Rice, per week, one half of which will consist of Bread or Biscuit (Potatoes will also be issued, at the rate of 5lbs. of Potatoes in lieu of 1lb. of Flour, Oatmeal, or Rice), and 3 quarts of Water per day. – Issued not less than twice a week.[35]

Notwithstanding inspection by government emigration agents, it was still possible for ship owners and captains to provide less than either the advertised, or the required amounts of food and water. Many horrendous accounts of voyages taken in the 1830s and 1840s testify to the adroitness and malevolence of those in charge. There is, however, no evidence that the Bensons' voyage was compromised by anything other than bad weather, delays and an occurrence of sickness. The *Sarah Stewart* crossed the Atlantic in six and a half weeks but it was not unusual for twice that amount of time to elapse and with such delay there came the problems of adequate food supply and scarcity of clean water.

Benson's description of the storm encountered three days out from Belfast is not fanciful. Ships departing Ireland at the commencement of the shipping season (late March or early April) sometimes encountered storms in the Irish Sea if they were travelling southwards from Belfast. Mid-Atlantic gales were common and being becalmed in fog off the Newfoundland shore often added further danger and time to the voyage. Threats of sickness and contagious disease were omnipresent. Crowded ships, poor ventilation and inadequate sanitary provision were inevitable discomforts but when stormy weather necessitated the closing of hatches and the confining of steerage passengers below decks for several consecutive days those discomforts expanded with devastating effect. Eight children took ill and one man died among Benson's fellow passengers. The mortality rate on this occasion was low and compared favourably with an estimated average mortality rate of around one percent.[36] It may have been an unpleasant voyage but it was probably no worse than most and was better than some. The captain of the *Sarah Stewart*, for example, had sufficient surplus food and water to enable him to supply a stricken vessel encountered off Newfoundland, permitting it to resume its voyage to Liverpool. There is no account of anyone aboard the *Sarah Stewart* suffering food deprivation.

All sixteen ships that sailed from Belfast with their complements of passengers in 1841 made it safely to Quebec City and there is no record of any of the vessels experiencing exceptional mortality levels during their voyage. Not all emigrants had such an uneventful crossing. In 1841 *The Quebec Mercury* noted:

> Limerick passenger ships have been particularly unfortunate this season. It was only in May last that we had to report the loss of The Minstrel from that port with about 160 passengers, when 137 of them, with 11 of the crew, unfortunately perished [and] the Bark Amanda ex Limerick for Quebec came ashore at Little Metis Point on 26th Sept. 29 passengers and 12 crew lost: 10 passengers and 6 crew saved.[37]

In the same vein, a fellow Ulsterman, William Campbell, who travelled from Belfast to Quebec City in the summer of 1839 experienced a horrendous voyage, even though he was a medical doctor and could afford a cabin on deck of the *Billy Booth*. In a letter to his father in Templepatrick, Co. Antrim, Campbell recalled the nightmare conditions that arose on board very soon after they left the shelter of Belfast Lough.

> We left Belfast Lough on Sunday morning the 1st of July and the day following the work of death commenced. The first death was that of an old man of cholera mortus … then came Tuesday when our carpenter lay down, affected in the same manner … Then four of the sailors took badly, I think merely from imagination, and the passengers began to take alarm. Some would have the Capt. to put into harbour, others wished to proceed. The storm arose and the winds blew direct in our teeth. The captain cursed so that he might have been heard distinctly on the coast of Waterford, although some leagues off. All was battle and confusion. I was as busy as a gravedigger, sometimes in the cabin, then in the steerage and often in the forecastle. The sickness prevailed for the space of twelve weeks and before our anchorage at Quebec we had no less than 24 deaths, mostly from cholera. The captain took it himself the very night we anchored at Grosse Isle.[38]

The quarantine station at Grosse Isle had been opened in 1832 in response to the large numbers of cholera-ridden immigrants arriving from Europe at that time. It continued to serve as a quarantine and immigration station for the next one hundred years before being converted into an animal testing and quarantine base. More recently the island has been designated by

Parks Canada as the Irish Memorial National Historic Site, an evocative tribute to the thousands of Irish emigrants who died on the island during the famine years. The Bensons being in good health, were not required to enter quarantine on the island and, probably with some relief, he recorded "Arrived at Quarantine, we passed the same day, on our way to Montreal."[39]

As they sailed up the St Lawrence Wilson was struck by the physical and cultural landscapes evident from the boat but he refrained from detailing the scene "the beauties of which have been so frequently described by abler pens than mine."[40] That scene would have presented a landscape very foreign to his experience. The broad sweep of the river, several kilometres wide in parts, the strings of French Canadian agricultural villages, the numerous tin-roofed Catholic churches and the looming Laurentian mountains in the background introduced visitors to the distinctive landscape of Quebec, formerly New France. Lord Dufferin, to whom Benson dedicated his autobiography, arrived from Ulster to take up the position of Governor General of Canada in 1872. Even he, notwithstanding his many travels around the world, was forcibly struck by the uniqueness of the Quebec landscape visible from vessels on the river.

> One's first view of a new continent is always as an epoch in one's life. What struck me most were the primaeval woods which covered the hills at Gaspe for miles and miles through the interior. One felt one saw what the first red Adam and Eve first opened their eyes upon.[41]

The Quebec Mercury recorded the arrival of the *Sarah Stewart* on 22 May 1841 with 274 passengers. This was one more than the complement on leaving Belfast but it is possible that either a late correction was made to the numbers or a birth had taken place on board. There was no mention of the death of the passenger at sea that Benson remembered. The port of Quebec City had opened for the new shipping season on May 1 that year with the arrival of a ship from London; the captain of that vessel reported considerable ice on the Grand Banks. The captain of a ship from Glasgow confirmed the lingering presence of ice in the Gulf of St Lawrence on May 4 and it was not until two weeks later that transatlantic vessels began to arrive in significant numbers. Over one hundred ships arrived at the port of Quebec City from May 16 to 18. Among them was a vessel from Waterford carrying only ballast. The first ship directly from Ireland carrying passengers was the *Tottenham* from New Ross. It arrived on May 19 with a complement of eighty-three emigrants. Benson and his wife arrived one week later and were among the first Irish to disembark at Quebec that year. In the week of their arrival (May 21 to 25) a total of eighty-six vessels discharged at the port; twelve of those ships had originated in Ireland and among them they carried a total of 2,228 passengers in steerage, a remarkable tally for a single week in a season that was not especially noted for being a crisis period in emigration.[42]

The 1841 shipping season proved to be the busiest for several years. A total of 1,251 ships arrived from Britain, Ireland, the USA and the Caribbean. More than 28,000 passengers (almost sixty percent of them directly from Ireland) disembarked in a city whose permanent population at the time did not exceed 31,000. The deep-water port of Quebec City was the third largest port in North America in terms of tonnage, and its water and shore-based activities were concentrated in a shipping season that lasted little more than six months, being attenuated in both spring and winter by thick floes of ice on the St Lawrence.[43] These climatological conditions limited the window of opportunity for emigration from Ireland and, as Figure 2.1 demonstrates, virtually three-quarters of immigrants arrived in the months of May and June. Correspondingly, the busiest months for departures from Ireland were April and May. Few ship owners risked commencing the westward voyage beyond the beginning of August although, unusually, the *Champlain* did depart Youghal on September 1, arriving at Quebec City at the close of the shipping season on October 20 with a load of ballast and seven passengers. It was the *Champlain's* second Atlantic crossing that season for it had previously arrived on May 20 with fifty-two passengers but such logistical feats were most unusual. No ship with passengers on board sailed from Ireland in 1841 before April 2; the Bensons were among the earliest to leave and Wilson's recorded date of March 28 is improbable. Nonetheless, the fact that he and his wife were aboard the first ship to leave Belfast for Quebec City that season does confirm that they had planned their departure well in advance and were well organised for the journey.

Five days after arrival at Quebec City the *Sarah Stewart* transferred to the loading docks in the port and on June 26, just over a month after arrival, it was cleared for a voyage to Dublin with an unspecified cargo that, presumably, consisted mostly of timber and wheat.[44] H.N. Jones had chartered the vessel for the eastward leg of the voyage. Upon arrival in Dublin it was unloaded and eventually sailed to its homeport of Belfast, although it may have done some work on the Irish Sea in the meantime. People and goods were ingredients in a bustling transatlantic shipping trade and owners sought to recoup their capital investment by keeping the ships in transit as much as possible. The emergence of mass migration was a welcome addition to the opportunities available to ship owners and mercantile firms, but it was a secondary function.

The primary function of the mercantile business was to convey Canadian colonial resources to the imperial core in Britain. All ships on the

Aug
7%

Sept Oct
1% 0%

July
7%

June
7%

April
52%

April
May
June
July
Aug
Sept
Oct

May
26%

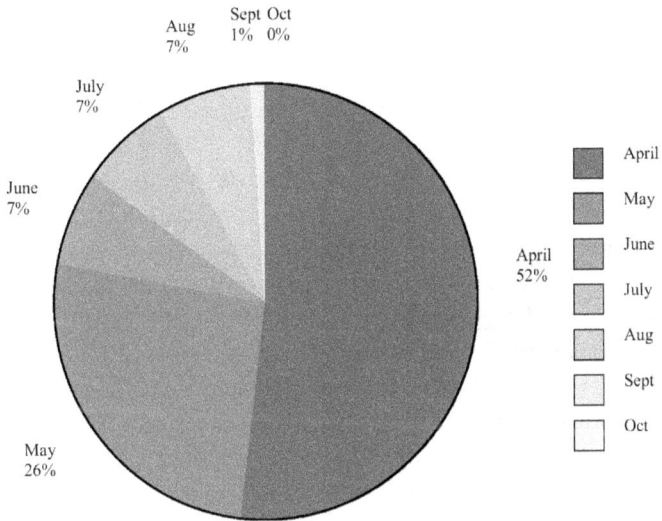

A   Month of Departure of Emigrants from Ireland to Quebec City, 1841

N = 16,173

Sept
4%

Oct April
1% 0%

Aug
9%

May
48%

April
May
June
July
Aug
Sept
Oct

July
20%

June
18%

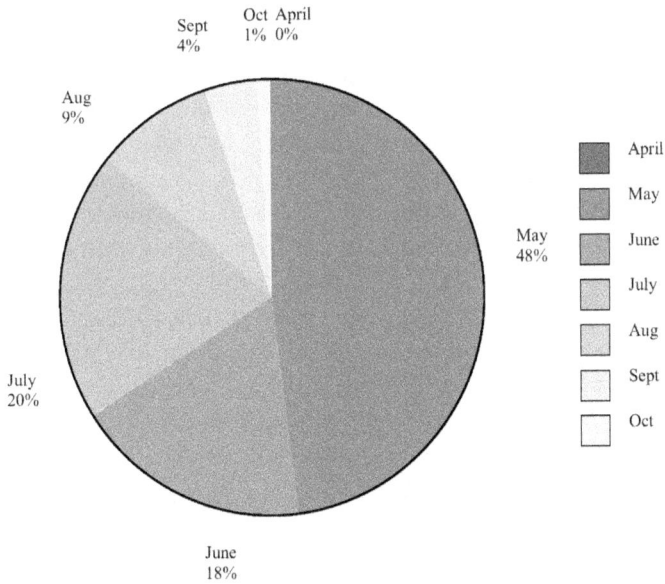

B   Month of Arrival at Quebec City of Immigrants from Ireland, 1841

Fig. 2.1: Months of departure of ships from Ireland
and their arrival in Quebec, 1841

35

westward leg of the voyage carried extensive tonnage of ballast; many carried only ballast. It was this spare capacity that facilitated continual expansion of the emigrant trade on converted cargo ships. Even during the peak of the Great Famine there was capacity to transport all who were able to afford the passage although the pressure of numbers did mean that even unworthy vessels were commandeered for the purpose. Not until the second half of the nineteenth century was a clear distinction established between cargo and passengers. Stimulated by stricter maritime regulations and a torrent of migrants from Europe, large-scale purpose-built passenger steamships emerged on the Atlantic route. Irish emigrant continued to occupy a disproportionately large share of that enlarged and more comfortable capacity. Henceforth disembarking passengers would be subjected to much more regulatory control than was the case when the Bensons arrived in the chaotic and bustling port of Quebec in late May, 1841.

The Journey Inland

Disembarking after their long ocean voyage the Bensons would have found themselves amid an unfamiliar bustling melee of port workers, hucksters, hotel-keepers and agents offering transport to other parts of the country. To all arrivals it was obvious that a new and challenging land awaited them but for those intending to travel further westward to English-speaking Upper Canada (later Ontario) another stage had to be completed. Wilson and his wife had selected Kingston as their destination, a city some five hundred kilometres southwest of Quebec City and three hundred kilometres from Montreal. Jemima's brother who lived in Hastings County about one hundred kilometres north of Kingston may have influenced their choice of destination but an additional important factor would have been the scale and importance of the town. In 1841 Kingston, located at the junction of Lake Ontario and the St Lawrence River and mid-way between Toronto and Montreal, was the largest urban centre in Upper Canada. Endowed with significant military, administrative and commercial structures it was a striking place and for a brief period, 1841–4, it served as the first capital of the united Canadas (represented by the union of Upper and Lower Canada).

Travelling by ship from Quebec City to Montreal, the Bensons then boarded a flat-bottomed Durham boat that was drawn by horses through the Lachine canal and upstream on the St Lawrence as far as Brockville. There they were scheduled to transfer to a lake steamer for the remaining eighty kilometres to Kingston.[45] This set of logistical arrangements was an expensive finale to the emigration adventure and it proved too much for Benson's remaining funds. At the last moment he decided to remain in Brockville rather than Kingston and after paying for a single night's lodgings he was destitute. Brockville, with a population of 2,000, was an important regional commercial and administrative centre, well established as a transfer point for steamers and immigrants coming along the river. Fine stone buildings encircled the town's green where the district court, jail, and customs offices were located along with the main churches, schools, two banks, and several factories. The landscape, shadowed by forest and dominated by the presence of the heavily trafficked St. Lawrence River was well captured in a sketch by contemporary artist, Frederick H. Holloway (Figure 2.2). The town was heavily engaged in conservative politics and it was there that Ogle R. Gowan, an immigrant from Wexford, had founded The Grand Orange Lodge of British North America in 1830. By the time of Benson's arrival, Orangemen were numerous in the town and its hinterland: Orange celebrations were a regular occurrence.

The town had some potential for the employment and Benson had no money to travel further, being reduced to sleeping in the local graveyard for several nights. For the time being, he had reached the end of his journey. A new and challenging life awaited him and in meeting those challenges he would draw upon the skills, resources and experiences acquired during the formative first twenty years of his life in Ulster.

Fig. 2.2: Brockville c. 1841, looking up the St Lawrence River,
from the lower end of Brockville as sketched by Frederick H. Holloway

Notes and References

1 Cecil J. Houston and William J. Smyth, *Irish Emigration and Canadian Settlement, Patterns, Links and Letters* (Toronto and Belfast: University of Toronto Press and Ulster Historical Foundation, 1990), 76–119.

2 For a discussion of the nature of the global Irish diaspora see C.J. Houston and W.J. Smyth, "The Irish Diaspora: Emigration to The New World, 1720–1820" in B.J. Graham and L.J. Proudfoot (eds), *An Historical Geography of Ireland* (London: Academic Press, 1993), 338–60.

3 A recent survey of that migration history may be found in William J. Smyth, "Ireland and Northern Ireland" in Klaus J. Bade, Pieter C. Emmer, Leo Lucassen and Jochen Oltmer (eds), *The Encyclopedia of Migration and Minorities in Europe, From The Seventeenth Century to The Present* (Cambridge: Cambridge University Press, 2011), 27–33.

4 Houston and Smyth, *Irish Emigration*, 66.

5 Benson, 99.

6 Benson, 102.

7 Lloyd's *Register of Ships*, 1845.

8 Benson, 101.

9 Benson, 102.

10 *The Quebec Mercury*, May 25, 1841.

11 Appendix no. 7 to Minutes of Evidence, Report From The Select Committee of The House of Lords On Colonisation From Ireland, session 19 January–23 July 1847, vol. vi. 1847.

12 *The Belfast Newsletter*, April 9, 1841. Microfilm copy of this is held in the Public Record Office of Northern Ireland.

13 We are indebted to Professor T.F. McIlwraith of the University of Toronto for sharing his unpublished research on ship ballast. In general, little is known about the nature and specific origins of the ballast loaded onto ships in Belfast at the time. The need for ballast diminished greatly when shipping moved from sail to steam power and as a consequence carried considerable tonnage of coal.

14 Data for the number of ships, their passenger complement and cargo details are derived from *The Quebec Mercury*, 1841.

15 William A. Spray, "Reception of the Irish in New Brunswick" in P.M. Toner (ed.), *New Ireland Remembered: Historical Essays on the Irish in New Brunswick* (Fredericton: New Ireland Press, 1988), 11–29.

16 The original and most analytical research on these figures remains that of William Forbes Adams, *Ireland and Irish Emigration to the New World, From 1815 to the Famine* (New Haven: Yale University Press, 1932).

17 For a review of the scale of emigration to Canada at this time see Houston and Smyth, *Irish Emigration*, 13–79.

18 In 1836 the British Parliament authorised the construction of a railway from Belfast to Armagh city. The first train arrived in Lisburn on August 12, 1839. However, the line was not extended to Portadown until January 31, 1842, ten months after the Bensons had travelled to Belfast.

19 Benson, 100.

20 Benson, 99.

21 James Humphrey's letter from Highland Creek, Ontario, to his parents in Co. Londonderry, September 24, 1824. Copy held by Public Record Office of Northern Ireland.

22 Details of this advertisement are available on Irish Emigration Database, Dippam (www.dippam.ac.uk), accessed online November 13, 2013.

23 Gerald J.J. Tulchinsky and Alan R. Dever, "Ryan Thomas" in *Dictionary of Canadian Biography*, vol. xi (Toronto: University of Toronto Press, 1982).

24 Adams, *Ireland and Irish*, 181.

25 Benson, 102.

26 Alexander Buchanan, the British emigration agent stationed in Quebec, expressed this view in 1839. Buchanan's comments are discussed in some detail in William Forbes Adams, *Ireland and Irish*, 221.

27 The Carruthers who emigrated from Co. Fermanagh to Canada in the 1840s arranged for seed from their home meadow and flower seed from the garden to be brought out to their farm in Ontario. Houston and Smyth, *Irish Emigration*, 254.

28 Marguerite M. Fallona, *Fallona–Kelly 1750–1990: A Study of Two Irish Families with a Guide To Sources For Research* (Belfast: Ulster Historical Foundation, 1996), 53.

29 Details of the barque are provided by Lloyd's *Register of Ships*, 1836.

30 *The Quebec Mercury*, January 2, 1841.

31 For a detailed discussion on the nature of the relationship between Irish merchants and Canadian ship builders see Cecil J. Houston and William J. Smyth, "New Brunswick Shipbuilding and Irish Shipping: The Commissioning of the Londonderry, 1838", in *Acadiensis*, vol. xvi, no. 2, 1987, 95–107.

32 Lloyd's *Register of Ships*, 1842, 1845 and 1846.

33 Edwin C.Guillet, T*he Great Migration: The Atlantic Crossing By Sailing Ship, 1770–1860* (Toronto: University of Toronto Press 1972), 15.

34 Ibid., 14.

35 Details of this advertisement are available on Irish Emigration Database, Dippam (www.dippam.ac.uk), accessed November 13, 2013.

36 Guillet, *The Great Migration*, 17.

37 *The Quebec Mercury*, October 5, 1841.

38 Letter from William Campbell, Ontario, to his father in Templepatrick, Co. Antrim, October 28, 1839. Public Record Office of Northern Ireland.

39 Benson, 102.

40 Ibid.

41 Letter from Lord Dufferin, Riviere-Du-Loup, Quebec, to the Duchess of Argyle, August 3, 1872. Public Record Office of Northern Ireland.

42 The figures for the arrival of ships are to be found in various copies of *The Quebec Mercury*, May 1841.

43 Cole Harris, *The Reluctant Land: Society, Space and Environment in Canada Before Confederation* (Vancouver: University of British Columbia Press, 2008), 268.

44 *The Quebec Mercury*, June 26, 1841.

45 The Lachine Canal was built in 1825 as a means of bypassing the Lachine rapids that prevented boats from Montreal accessing the upstream section of the St Lawrence River. The canal was fifteen kilometres in length and serviced by seven locks.

3

Settling in: Wilson Benson and the Canadian Frontier, 1840–70

The Canadian colony was in an immature state when the recently wed Bensons arrived in the spring of 1841 and in common with most other immigrants they faced considerable challenges in navigating the new society. In their favour, they did have the comfort of the English language, familiar British institutions and a general sense of cultural affinity and the reassuring community of Irish faces and accents. The place, however, was in flux; unfinished and unpolished. In Upper Canada (Ontario) towns were small and scattered mainly along the northern bank of the St Lawrence and the northern shores of Lakes Ontario and Erie. Much of the better lands south of the rugged granite outcrops of the Canadian Shield had been allocated to settlers and speculative land companies and there remained only limited opportunity to obtain a free grant of land. Farms could be purchased but that required some capital. Even then farmsteads were primitive, transportation networks basic and the landscape bore all the marks of recent and rudimentary forest clearance. New traditions, many of them imported from the United States, were in the throes of being introduced for coping with forest clearance, building log shanties and establishing a base for crop husbandry; tasks in which immigrants from the British Isles were singularly unskilled.

American, Scottish, English and Irish immigrants, as well as descendants of Empire Loyalists who had fled northwards after the American Revolution blended their aspirations in a new setting: friction was not unknown. In the more recent pioneering districts the Irish were prominent, as they had formed the majority among immigrants in the second quarter of the nineteenth century. In bringing an Irish sensibility to the frontier they also recreated some of the same conflicts familiar in Ireland. In Upper Canada at least two-thirds of the Irish were Protestant in religion, very many of them of Ulster origin, and their settlement pattern was more ubiquitous than that of their Catholic counterparts who were often concentrated in particular townships. Benson encountered some of these complexities rather quickly. He also acquired new skills and perspectives, ultimately preparing him to negotiate and invest in the country. He took about eight years to embrace the emerging nation and commit to being a Canadian.

By the 1840s the frontier of Upper Canada was in a late phase of the English imperial drive to populate its North American colonies and extract strategic timber resources. The colony had been under development since the 1780s when Loyalists from the American Revolution initiated settlement along the St Lawrence, on the Niagara peninsula between Lakes Ontario and Erie, and in the southwest beside the French settlement at the Detroit frontier. The Loyalists had sustained a war with the United States during 1812–14, then welcomed the first waves of transatlantic immigrants uprooted by economic collapse. Together they lived through their share of economic recessions on the Canadian side and helped turn back the rebellions that broke out in 1837 in both the Upper and Lower colonies. In the aftermath, the Colonial Office in London united Canada's Lower and Upper Colonies in 1841, renaming them Canada East (later known as Quebec) and Canada West (later known as Ontario). Benson and thousands of others arrived at a formative moment in the creation of Canada. As indicated by observations in his narrative he seemed to understand the ramifications of the recent rebellions and the formative moment of political challenge, but like most of his fellow immigrants he was focused on making a living and finding the niche that emigration promised.

In the early 1840s, the Bensons and their fellow newcomers entered a stalled economy and an unsettled political situation. They encountered an untidy mixed landscape of small open clearings among vistas of forest that extended over six hundred kilometres from Montreal to the western end of Lake Ontario, and from there another three hundred kilometres to Detroit. Northward limits extended between one and two hundred kilometres inland from the Great Lakes. In advance of the settlers, surveyors had traversed much of the forest and determined the straight-line boundaries of property lots and rights-of-way for roads. The distribution of lands from the Crown to the public for exploitation was a well-practiced process. Developed during the plantations of Ireland and Virginia in the seventeenth century, and applied too in the new settlements of eastern Europe and Russia, most settlers knew how it worked, and the Irish most definitely. It required settlers who would proclaim their loyalty and also move from their homes to settle abroad.

Timber, and later wheat exports, drove the colonial economy. The great pine trees were felled and squared to provide fine timber for British markets and colonial building projects. They were floated and rafted down rivers toward Ottawa, Belleville and Prescott, past Brockville and Montreal, eventually reaching the port of Quebec City where they were loaded for shipment across the Atlantic. Every facet of the timber trade depended on people in motion. Wage labourers moved from site to site and local settlers were engaged concurrently in travel between forests and fields, between clearing the forest and tending crops. Scatterings of clearings of a few to several acres slowly appeared among the trees and were extended by a couple of acres or more each year – eventually creating wide expanses of agricultural land. A mobile population sustained the expanding geography of this vast patchwork and laid the foundations of settlement. Among the dishevelled and cluttered vistas of incomplete fields, rough fences, intractable boulders, and innumerable stumps of the former forest, the immigrants had stepped back to an earlier phase of rural progress. It would take at least two generations to clear the land and perhaps another to groom the topography left by the retreat of the ice some 12,000 years before. Today, on the farm that Benson settled, the bottom fields covering about twenty acres have still not been completely groomed. They were cleared of their trees and brush, left to grow grass for rough pasture, and still bear the pocked and pitted surface remaining from the glacial past. Though thinned regularly for firewood and building timber, vestiges of forest, often covering between a tenth and a third of the space would remain on most farms.[1]

Obtaining land was the first step in attaining the stability dreamt of by most settlers and by 1841 most of the land was not free. It required considerable capital to purchase farm lots or pay the fees and charges required for settlement duties, and although some brought capital with them many settlers had to build savings on the Canadian side. In addition, capital was required for the purchase of tools and equipment, livestock and a food supply capable of sustaining the family until the first crops were harvested. It has been estimated that approximately £50 was required to equip a settler taking up a land grant – more if partially cleared land had to be purchased. At the time, an agricultural labourer could hope to earn £30 per annum and would therefore require some time before attempting to acquire a farm.

Besides the need for cash, acquisition of a farm required specific knowledge of where land was available and the relevant terms and conditions of settlement, including the application procedure. Documents designated as location tickets were issued in government land offices in settlement districts and towns, or at the offices of a quasi-governmental agency like the Canada Land Company. The location tickets assigned a lot of land that had already been surveyed and prescribed duties that a settler had to complete before a deed known as "a patent" could be issued. The duties usually amounted to clearing about five acres, planting them in crops, building a house and living in it for a prescribed time. The system did not guarantee that any lot would be useful or profitable for settlers but those settlers who were most familiar with the arrangements could take advantage of the rules. To minimize risks, a cautious settler might first visit the area under development and consider the various sites on offer and then return to the land office and claim a specific ticket before venturing back to start clearing. However, it was difficult to predict future soil fertility and, apart from general advice to avoid swampy and rocky areas, there was a considerable element of luck involved. Vacant lots, inhospitable terrain and the slow incremental pace of settlement meant that pioneer settlers had few close neighbours. Community formation was further impeded by initial difficulties in transportation.

Even in the 1840s roads were barely passable. They existed as rough tracks meandering around roots, boulders, and swamps. Their surfaces were scarcely levelled and under the rain and drying winds any attempt at grading did not last long. Well-sprung carriages might challenge the ruts but a wagon for distant travel was rarely recommended. Travel by sleigh over frozen winter snow was an easier mode of transportation.[2] Villages appeared in clearings at the junctions of roads and rivers where a grain-mill might be built. A rudimentary village might appear overnight and almost as quickly disappear because better locations were developed and the pattern of settlements altered. Some of the more central villages grew into enduring towns under the guidance of colonial administrators and entrepreneurs. Along the north shore of the St Lawrence and Lake Ontario several substantial towns had emerged: Cornwall, Brockville, Kingston, Belleville, Port Hope, Coburg, Toronto, Dundas and Hamilton. These places served as staging areas for immigrants moving westwards, northward and inland and they proved especially critical in assisting the large inflow of Irish immigrants in the post-Napoleonic phase of immigration. In each of these towns significant Irish communities were established. Likewise Bytown (Ottawa) on the Ottawa River and at the terminus of the Rideau Canal was a significant immigrant staging area and had several outlying timber districts where Irish labourers could find work.

For much of the year, boats plying river and lake routes guided settlers inland and eased the difficulties of travelling across land. In the seventeenth and eighteenth centuries the French had demonstrated the efficiency of river and lake travel by connecting Montreal with their settlement at Detroit. Early in the British settlement, schooners and scows moved timber and building materials as well as immigrants around Lake Ontario. Canadian ports and their American counterparts traded across the border in foodstuffs and livestock and those connections also served immigrants. By 1832, the Rideau Canal connected Kingston and Bytown and the

Welland Canal, with its impressive lock system capable of moving ships across the Niagara escarpment between Lakes Ontario and Erie, was in operation. These developments opened travel to Lake Huron and well beyond. Several steamship companies operated between the main towns and were crucial for the westbound immigrant traffic from Montreal. A vibrant trading system steadily increased the capacity to move immigrants and by 1840 the Great Lakes frontier assumed a reality and prominence on the ground that had initially only existed in concept on a map. Lake, canal and river transportation was central to Benson's initial attempts to secure employment and in the years 1843–9 he served as cook, and general deck hand on several steamers. He turned his attention to peddling fish, vegetables, milk, whiskey and other goods during the winter months when navigation was halted by ice on the river and in the lakeside ports.

Wilson and Jemima, having grown up in north Armagh among a dense population and congested landscape of houses, hedged lanes, and tiny and irregular farm fields, could not have imagined the low population densities, ragged appearance and rough condition of their new world. For immigrants, the living conditions in the settled districts were rarely reassuring. Roughly built shanties were typical and strewn across the landscape, sheltering families of the poor and the "middling" classes. Arguably, however, these early and rudimentary shelters were no worse than the cramped and basic conditions provided for the cottier and weaving populations of Ulster. In time, better log cabins, timber frame and stone houses replaced the shanties and signalled a discernible degree of improvement. The best Canadian country farmhouses and town residences of professionals could measure well against their old country counterparts but underdeveloped rudimentary surroundings prevailed for some time. The towns, emulating the Georgian and Gothic themes of the then contemporary English urban architecture, held out an older vision of a future that many emigrants had already left behind.[3] To be in Canada in 1841 was to be present at the early stages of a new society building itself in the image of what the immigrants had known at home, substituting the locally available timber for the stone and mud that had provided the building material in Ireland.

Social institutions emerged early in the colony but like the landscape some were quite rudimentary. The English government had transferred to the colony all the structures and limitations required to keep the colony British. The royal commander held the office of Lieutenant Governor and was appointed by London, an arrangement familiar to the immigrants as practically all of them had originated in Britain and Ireland. English laws, the legislative assembly, courts and the requisite offices and officers guaranteed the usual rights of British subjects. Enslavement had ended in

1833 and several hundred people of African and aboriginal origin had also attained those rights. The Canadian colony had become the end point on the Underground Railway for fugitive African-American slaves and Benson recounted helping a runaway slave escape from Pennsylvania, smuggling him northwards across Lakes Erie and Ontario to his freedom in Toronto. All state institutions initially assumed an English model but in time adjustments were made to accommodate the basic English-French compromise underpinning the country. The future province of Ontario emerged as British and would not deviate from that identity during Wilson's lifetime.

Community organisations demonstrated all the complexity of their Old World origins. Although the survey system spread people out in one hundred acre parcels of land, specifically created to allow families to establish an independent and economically viable agricultural holding, the need for company and community brought people together in groupings that were familiar reconstructions of those in the old world. The importance of religious worship and fellowship, socialising and conviviality were crucial to creating a bearable life on the frontier and settlers found simple ways to enliven and warm their existence. Churches functioned as the main community organizations and all major Christian denominations were represented. The Church of England was pre-eminent in the colony: Methodism thrived, supported by circuit riders and mobile preachers who attracted many former Anglicans and Presbyterians to its ranks. The Catholic Church, predominantly associated with the Irish in regions outside of Quebec, catered to a minority and even after the Relief Act of 1829 the Protestant majority continued to view it with suspicion. Slowly, parishes and territorial districts for church attendance were created and an ecclesiastical order was grafted on to the administrative cadastral divisions of the counties and townships. On a more secular front, Orange halls were built as community centres from an early stage in the settlements. Schools, privately run inns, and taverns appeared in many communities from the first days but commercial entertainment was rare in the rural districts.

Politico-religious animosity between Protestants and Catholics, honed amid the sectarian atmosphere of Ulster, was transferred to Upper Canada and an Orange–Catholic abrasion was apparent in many early settlements. However, the context had changed greatly. Many more groups and interests intervened and the diversity tended to remove the singularity of focus on sectarian matters and dampened the ferocity of Irish antipathies. Even so, parochial and regional loyalties fostered in the old country defined many of the new colony's social circumstances. Emigration did not end disputes but it often modified their Canadian versions.[4] Not all conflicts were delineated along religious and ethnic divisions; regional and group identities were also a source of friction, especially among workers labouring on the canals. Observing the construction of the Cornwall and Beauharnois canals on the St Lawrence River, Benson described a riot between Irish immigrant labourers from Cork and Connaught respectively:[5]

> The former, being the most numerous, obtained the mastery. News of this reached the Cornwall works; the Connaught men here, who were most numerous, determined to avenge the cause of their party, and drove the handles out of their picks, and with other bludgeons fell upon the Cork men ... My countrymen earned for themselves an unenviable notoriety and produced an impression, especially among the rural population of Canada at that time, that the Irish, one and all, were hard cases.

In this new frontier environment, mobility was a central feature of life. There was no assumption that anyone could arrive and prosper on the spot wherever they first settled down. People with some capital, an established trade or profession might settle quickly into available opportunities. Some had the means to take over "start-up farms" or begin new ones and hire help. Some would move on in search of cheaper land and larger units that could be found inland, away from the lake. Mobility was the most common theme and outcome of the settlement process. Tradesmen also had to be mobile as few places were sufficiently large and established to provide steady work for many. For the general labouring classes, work was ever a challenge and life was marked by searches to find employment and acquire new skills. The immature economy, the economic rhythms of growth and decline, and the extreme seasonality of most productive activities all contributed to intense geographical mobility. Benson found himself among the general labouring classes. Early efforts to familiarize themselves with the possibilities of their new land kept him and his wife on the move; identifying opportunities and acquiring work, much of it temporary and seasonal in nature. In Scotland, Wilson had learned the necessity of mobility and opportunism in his search for a living; his Canadian experience was much of the same but the distances were greater and the development stages more crude.

The Bensons' First Decade in Canada

In their first years in Canada, Wilson and Jemima's lives were indeed very mobile. In Brockville, Benson set immediately to finding work and reverted to practices he adopted with his sister during their trip to Scotland. Jemima was hired out to do general housework and dressmaking and in return receive room and board while he tramped the roads around town and into the countryside in search of work. Countless thousands of immigrants started their Canadian journeys that way. He slept nine nights in the town's cemetery and another out of town curled in a fence corner. Unprepared for the demands of the local economy and deemed unskilled, he found it difficult to access employment and was thus forced to keep on the move. He eventually contracted to weave a web of woollen cloth and obtained a farm labouring stint that was meant to last a month, but was terminated within a week, and received only seventy-five cents pay. He became a porter at a main street hotel and then tried his hand at baking and confectioning, a job that allowed him to see Jemima daily.[6] He worked as a baker for six months and probably survived his first winter because of it. He then agreed to serve as a shoemaker's apprentice but that lasted only two days. General labouring work followed in an agricultural implements factory and he was able to carry that through the winter of 1843.[7] Meanwhile Jemima was still engaged in dressmaking and together by the spring of 1843 they had managed to save $60–70. These savings could have bought them a small farm or a house in the town, but they avoided those decisions.

Wilson thought of returning to Ireland for he had not yet obtained in Canada a trade that would serve him better than weaving. His main work, and Jemima's too, rested in urban activities and semi-skilled artisanal occupations and occasional peddling. In the spring of 1843 he signed on as cook for the steamer *Brockville* that plied the St Lawrence between the town and the eastern limit of navigation at Dickinson's Landing near Cornwall. At the end of the shipping season the couple left Brockville for Kingston and rented a house there in which Jemima could run a small grocery and general store. In summer, Wilson went to work on the steamers and in the winter he joined Jemima in operating the store. In Kingston Jemima gave birth to her first child, John. In the next year, however, Kingston lost its role as colonial capital to Montreal and slowly its economy and opportunities wilted. Wilson extended his world to Bytown, on the steamers' circle route downriver along the St Lawrence River, up the Ottawa River to Bytown, and back down the country through the Rideau Canal to Kingston. He expanded his trading range in groceries and foodstuffs, going as far afield on Lake Ontario as Belleville, about eighty kilometres west of Kingston. The family business of trading and peddling and seasonal work on the steamers kept him in the retail sector of the developing economy and moved him slowly westward. It also provided him with ample opportunity to get to know his new country and the social and economic skills required to prosper within it.

In 1847, then with a second child, the family left its base in Kingston and moved to Toronto (and perhaps Jemima's brother's family also went along). By then Toronto had outgrown the other towns along the north shore of Lake Ontario and its population had reached almost 30,000. In Toronto, Wilson and Jemima leased a small shop on Victoria Street in the heart of the city to sell goods locally and also ship fruit and vegetables to Kingston, using the differentials in prices between the two towns to sustain a profitable trade. Jemima obtained the goods and arranged their shipping down the lake. In Kingston Wilson sold the goods in the regular town market. By this date, they were well familiar with the retail rhythms of the colony and the logistics of steamer transportation.

The colony was overwhelmed in 1847 by the arrival of Famine immigrants seeking shelter and medical assistance. Deaths along the way in Grosse Isle, Montreal and Kingston were numbered in the thousands. About 38,000 emigrants reached Toronto where eventually over a thousand died and another two thousand chose to stay in the town.[8] Some of the remainder continued their journey west, congregating in the townships between Brantford and Niagara at the west end of Lake Ontario: very many headed south to the United States. While working on the steamer *Britannia*, Benson encountered many of the distressed migrants, noting: "during the season we had numbers of emigrants from the Old Country, many of whom were in a destitute condition and dying of fever. On several trips we have had two and three deaths between Montreal and Kingston."

In Canada the potato blight was also widespread and Wilson further noted "the rot had become so bad that a cask of potatoes shipped at Toronto on Saturday in apparently sound condition, were totally rotten when opened in Kingston on Monday following ..."[9] This part of his autobiography is rather tangled. He cites 1846 for the immigrant deaths on the *Britannia* when it was most likely 1847. Although the tangle may not be unravelled, the content is clear and it does not detract from the narrative's direction and meaning.

Taking up Farming

Five years after his arrival Benson made his first foray into the Canadian property market with the purchase of an acre of land in Richmond Township north of Kingston in late 1846. He "erected a snug house, although in the beginning of winter, and opened a general grocery, which my wife attended, while I travelled through the country with a miscellaneous stock of wares." The venture ended in disaster a few months later when the property was seized by the sheriff to settle a debt incurred by the original vendor. Wilson, having neglected to obtain a deed for his acre of land, was evicted in a manner reminiscent of the fate that had befallen his father in Drumnasue almost twenty years earlier. An attempt to establish an urban dairy in Kingston and a grocery store in Toronto followed, but both ventures ended in disaster – his cow was killed in Kingston and his store in Toronto burnt down. Nonetheless it would appear that he had managed to attain a level of modest prosperity from "our several earnings [which] placed us in comfortable circumstances" and those earnings encouraged him to once more consider the acquisition of land.

He reassessed possibilities, and took the suggestion from Jemima's brother to consider farming in the vicinity of Orangeville, a village some eighty kilometres northwest of Toronto. On this occasion he adopted a more cautious and informed approach. Jemima and her brother travelled to Orangeville with a barrel of whiskey to sell to cover the expenses of the journey and also to test the potential for sales in the area. They reported back positively about the settlement prospects. At the same time, Wilson in Toronto had received a letter informing him of his father's death in Ireland. Now that he was released from any further responsibilities in his homeland he prepared his next steps. He had learned enough about Canada to want to be part of its future; his longing to return to Ireland had faded and he was now committed to spending the rest of his life in the new country. Benson and his brother-in-law identified an unoccupied Clergy Reserve lot of 200 acres that had recently become available in the township of Amaranth. They had enough experience to recognise an opportunity about which recently arrived immigrants might not have been aware. Originally, government policy had required that one-seventh of all land should be set aside for the maintenance of the Anglican clergy. This seventh was allocated throughout the colony in 200-acre lots and such subsidization of the Anglican Church was a source of political controversy. The policy was abandoned in 1827 and subsequently Clergy Reserve lands were systematically released for sale to intending settlers. It is not clear how Wilson acquired his particular holding and it is possible that he may simply have squatted on the vacant lot.

Benson occupied the Clergy Reserve and commenced his first effort to make a farm. He had been eight years in the colony and had learned through observation how he might take advantage of this opportunity. He cleared bush and sowed crops, built a shanty, kept pigs and lived through bad weather and frozen crops. He survived a severe foot wound from chopping and braved the presence of bears and wolves. He worked for other farmers, haying and harvesting in the older, more developed zones and sold whiskey. He was debt-adverse and proudly recalled that he avoided most of the financial ills that beset Canadian settlers and drove them "to another section of country to conclude the farce of Hewers of Wood and Drawers of Water".[10] His text does not make it clear how long he spent at this activity.

The timing and duration of the Amaranth episode is unclear and, once

Fig. 3.1: Wilson Benson's Location Ticket, Artemesia Township, 1851

more, he seems to telescope experiences. His settling in Amaranth commenced at the end of the shipping season of 1849 and ended on a date he identified as February 14, 1851. Between those dates only one growing season existed, but his descriptions of the wheat crops in Amaranth suggest he may have been engaged in three crops at least, the first of which froze, and the second and third for which he was pleased to report success. At any rate, he sold his improvements on the Amaranth Clergy lot for $40 and moved again in February 1851, deep in the winter, to the forests of the Township of Artemesia, seventy kilometres farther west in the Queen's Bush, one of the last regions of free grant land of reasonable agricultural quality to be released for settlement in the region. He may have noticed *Smith's Canadian Gazetteer* reporting in 1846 that Artemesia "… is only just laid out, and is not yet opened for sale".[11] Benson invested in tools, draught animals, and many other supplies and headed towards the farm lot that would be his home for the next quarter of a century.

In 1851 Wilson obtained from the crown a "location ticket" to occupy a fifty-acre free grant of forested land. (Figure 3.1) The location ticket was

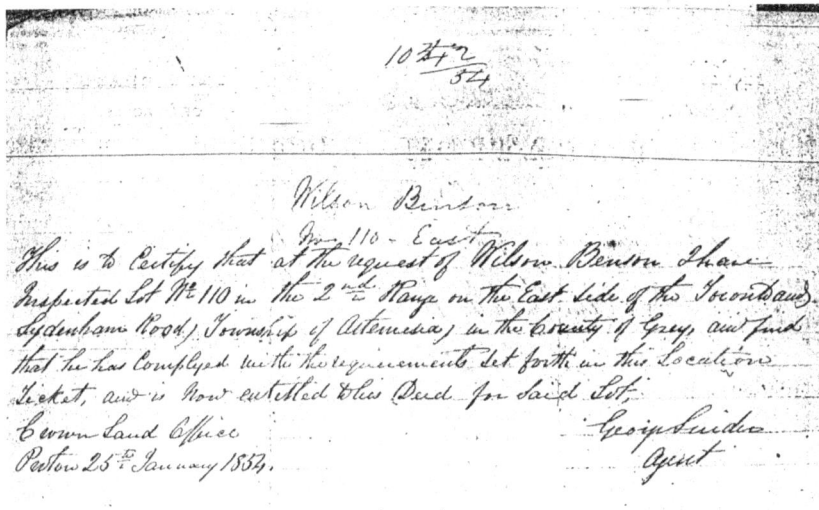

Fig. 3.2: Land Patent, 1854, granted to Benson confirming
his fulfillment of the terms of the original Location Ticket

issued February 28, 1851, two weeks after his departure from Amaranth,
and assigned him the rights to settle in Artemesia township on Lot No. 110
of the second range east of the Toronto settlement road, one of three roads
pushed through by the government to encourage settlement in the Queen's
Bush. Wilson was required "to clear and place under Crop 12 Acres of the
land within 4 years of the date of this Ticket, build a house 18 feet by 20,
and to reside on the land until this settlement duty is performed." He was
allowed also to hold in reserve an adjacent fifty acres for future purchase at
a nominal price of $25. In 1851, he could not have been more fortunate.
His location ticket closed the unrelenting family search for a secure future
initiated a generation before when his father's business failed in Belfast.

His effort to pioneer was well planned. For his first season in Artemesia
he was very well prepared to avoid the common pitfalls in the settlement
process and was sufficiently resourced to survive the difficulties of moving
onto uncleared land:

> I had brought with me a year's provisions, which lasted me till the
> growth of my own crop the following summer. I also brought a yoke
> of steers, two cows, a heifer, and some pigs. Fodder was almost out of
> the question, and I barely succeeded in purchasing two hundred
> pounds of straw, giving each animal a small handful night and
> morning, the rest of subtenance [sic] depending entirely on browse.[12]

During the previous year he had visited his lot on thirteen occasions to
build a dwelling and commence clearing before bringing his family there.

Not every settler had Benson's experience and foresight, leaving their house building to a later stage. Benson's first house was a single room log dwelling but sometime during the 1850s he replaced it with a one-and-a-half storey frame building although he makes no mention of it in his narrative.[13] Building the house was an important step in a family's establishment and a community's creation. In Canada West log houses were common, sometimes built as a second dwelling in replacement for the rough shanty or tent used during the first months. For some families, shanties lasted years. Logs were heavy and construction generally required the help of neighbours and a team of oxen. Storing several chords of dried firewood was another essential. The house was the first locus of family security, a place to withstand the winter, a key place for socializing and developing a sense of belonging to the new districts.

Table 3.1

THE BENSON FAMILY, ARTEMESIA TOWNSHIP, CENSUS OF 1851

Name	Occupation	Birthplace	Religion	Age
Wilson	Farmer	Ireland	W. Methodist	27
Jemima		Ireland	W. Methodist	25
John		Ontario	"	9
Eliza Jane		Ontario	"	6
Jemima		Ontario	"	3
William		Ontario	"	2

By the time the census taker arrived in the spring of 1851 to enumerate him, Jemima, their four children, and the farm possessions, he could point to two acres under crops that had produced ten bushels of oats, twenty bushels of potatoes and thirty bushels of turnips. His stock recorded in the census included two oxen, a heifer and a cow; a complement that was missing the pigs originally brought with him and which he had probably slaughtered for food and for sale. He would claim in his published autobiography that "his first crop was excellent, and altogether the prospect in my new home was cheering". By 1854 the Bensons had completed their settlement duties: they had resided there for three years, they had a simple log house of at least 18 feet by 20 feet, and put twelve acres under crop, the precise acreage required in the contract of his location ticket. They were granted their 'patent' or deed for Lot 110, joined the ranks of freehold landowners, and rejoiced in having their first permanent home, thirteen years after arriving in the colony.[14] (Figure 3.2) They could claim also to be among the founders of the new County of Grey that had been formalised in 1852.

Slowly, Wilson and Jemima, their family and neighbours pushed back the edge of the "dense forest of nightland, interspersed with swamps, marshes, beaver-meadows and jungle" replacing it with the ecology of more familiar agricultural environment. They had settled and the spectre of incessant mobility and wandering slowly dissipated. During the 1850s Wilson added thirty acres to his cleared land, putting about twenty-two acres under crops and leaving ten for pasture. His oldest son John was able to help. By 1860 he had added eighteen bushels of peas and 200 bushels of spring wheat to his annual production and increased his annual production of oats, potatoes and turnips seven-fold from sixty bushels total in 1851 to 428 bushels in 1860. That same year he saved four tons of hay. All these improvements enabled him to keep four cows and ten other cattle, half a dozen sheep and half a dozen pigs. The stock also added to the work, requiring fencing to protect them, and keep them out of the forest. The family prepared 150 pounds of maple sugar and fifty yards of wool flannel. His neighbours had a similar mix of produce and livestock. Wilson had made good on his opportunity to settle but his world was about to change.

August of 1860 proved tragic. After a brief illness, Jemima died of dysentery and nine days later her youngest child, Isabella, aged 3, succumbed to what was noted in the census of 1861 as 'infantile cholera'. The family then comprised Wilson and six children: John, aged 18, Elizabeth 14, Sara Ann 13, Wilson 11, Jemima 8, and Dorothea, aged 5. In January 1862 Wilson married Agnes Shield and commenced a second family.[15] Agnes was about ten years his junior. A fellow immigrant from Ireland, she had arrived in Canada as a child in 1840[16] and at the time of her marriage she was employed in the household of the Bensons' family doctor. Wilson continued to clear land and in 1866 exercised his option to buy the reserve Lot 109 next to his original free grant, and thus doubled the size of his farm to 100 acres.

Table 3.2

THE BENSON FAMILY, ARTEMESIA TOWNSHIP, CENSUS OF 1871

Name	Occupation	Birthplace	Religion	Age
Wilson	Farmer	Ireland	Ch of England	49
Agnes		Ireland	"	35
William		Ontario	"	7
Thomas		Ontario	"	6
Robert		Ontario	"	5
Mary		Ontario	"	3
Henrietta		Ontario	"	2
Isabella		Ontario	"	2/12

By 1871, according to census documents, Agnes had borne six children. Wilson had sixty-five of his one hundred acres cleared of trees and had created a substantial farm. His farm produce that year amounted to 111 bushels of wheat, 80 bushels of barley, 150 bushels of oats, 20 bushels of peas, 90 bushels of potatoes and 40 bushels of turnips. In addition he had produced 50 lbs of butter, 215 lbs of wool and 34 yds of cloth. It was a typical mixed farming enterprise and one that would have allowed him to feed his family and also supply the local market. Nothing in his farm enterprise would have appeared strange to a farmer with comparable acreage in contemporary Ireland.

His family was among the respected pioneers of the district and his friendships extended to include the local notables. Just before Christmas in 1873 he was seriously injured while thrashing grain at his neighbour's barn. Tired, and not paying close attention to his safety, he caught his clothing on the turnbuckle of the drive shaft and was beaten to the ground several times before someone could stop the machine. Left with a permanently twisted arm and a severely damaged leg, Wilson sold the farm and invested the proceeds in having a shop built in the nearby town of Markdale about two kilometres away. The indenture that legalized the sale of his one hundred-acre farm in Artemesia Township recorded the sale to Alexander Mercer of Erin Township, Wellington County. The transaction price was $3,000, of which $2,000 was received in currency and the remaining $1,000 taken back as a ten-year mortgage.[17] After a life of unremitting toil as weaver, trader, and farm pioneer, Wilson stepped back from farming to seek a living in retailing merchandise, a skill that he had practiced and refined at intervals since his youthful sojourn in Scotland. Availing of the time required for recuperation, and encouraged by clergymen friends to relate the experiences of his life, he put pen to paper and in 1876 published the chronicle and memoir which is the subject of this volume.

Notes and References

1 Cole Harris, *The Reluctant Land: Society, Space and Environment in Canada Before Confederation* (Vancouver: UBC Press, 2008), 316–76.

2 Thomas F. McIlwraith, "The adequacy of Rural Roads In The Era Before Railways; An Illustration From Upper Canada", *The Canadian Geographer*, 14, 1970, 334–60.

3 For an excellent analysis of the vernacular architecture of rural Ontario see Thomas F. McIlwraith, *Looking for Old Ontario* (Toronto: University of Toronto Press, 1997).

4 For an analysis of the significance of the Orange Order in Ontario see Cecil J. Houston and William J. Smyth, *The Sash Canada Wore: A Historical Geography of the Orange Order in Canada* (Toronto: University of Toronto Press, 1980).

5 Benson, 109.

6 Lusher's Hotel in Brockville was operated at that time by Eric Lusher. Brockville History Album, *All About The History of Brockville, Ontario*. Web page accessed March 16, 2013.

7 In 1828 Benjamin Chaffey opened a machine shop in Brockville specializing in building tug boats suitable for towing rafts of timber downstream to Montreal and Quebec City. In 1832, while caring for Irish immigrants, Chaffey succumbed to cholera and was succeeded by his son, also named Benjamin (1806–67). It was he who was in charge of the factory when Benson was hired. Brockville History Album, *All About The History of Brockville, Ontario*. Web page accessed March 16, 2013.

8 Mark G. McGowan, *Death or Canada: The Irish Famine Migration To Toronto, 1847* (Toronto: Norvallis Publishing Inc., 2009). At that time Toronto had a population of less than 30,000. The 1851 census recorded its population as 30,775.

9 Benson, 114.

10 Benson, 120.

11 *Smith's Gazetteer,* 1846.

12 Benson, 124.

13 The existence of the frame house was noted in the census of 1861.

14 Ontario Provincial Archives, *Land Patents*, 1854.

15 Ontario Provincial Archives *Marriage Records*, 1862. The Benson family genealogy described Wilson's second wife as Nancy Rich due to a misreading of the marriage record. The original document bears a supervisor's tick mark that partially obliterates the name of his spouse. However, the full name is visible in the index to the record. This document also provides us with the name of Wilson's parents.

16 Information on the date of her arrival in Canada is derived from the census of 1901.

17 This information is recorded in a listing GS 2194#1343 held by the Ontario Provincial Archives.

4

Rural Stability
and the Urban Experience

By the 1870s much of the land in the Queen's Bush in Grey County had been allocated to settlers who had made substantial progress in clearing the forest and establishing agricultural enterprises based on a farming blend of livestock and crop cultivation. Family oriented neighbourhoods had emerged, signalling the transition to settled communities and a relatively stable society. The reshaping of the rural landscape and the development of an increasingly complex local economy may be seen also as metaphors for the transformation that was simultaneously taking place in Benson's life when he moved to the nearby town of Markdale which became his home for the next three and a half decades. He observed, and well understood, the significance of the contemporary transformation of that part of Ontario noting:

> At the time of writing things have changed – a market at our own door – the sound of railway and steam whistles, of mills and manufactories, where a few short years ago resounded the howl of the wolf. Innumerable villages, containing mills, manufactories and general stores of merchandize now mark the spot which was overgrown by dense forest trees fifteen or twenty years ago. The stride of prosperity made by the County of Grey, and indeed the country at large, has been gigantic; and it is a source of extreme gratification to me, as it no doubt will be to all the pioneers of my early days, that their sacrifice of worldly comfort and exposure to toil and suffering have so largely contributed to the development of our country and the welfare of succeeding generations.[1]

Benson's generation had realized its ambition for material progress and could rejoice in the possibilities passed on to their children. Steam power which had been a primary instrument of change in the domestic linen industry early in his life in Ireland now connected his Canadian locale with national and international markets.

The Irish Dimension

By the 1850s, when he had decided to try his fortune as a pioneer farmer, the geography of rural communities across Upper Canada was already well established. Overall, the Irish were the largest ethnic group: in very many townships they were the predominant element in the population.

By the time of the 1871 census, in an expanse of territory that stretched over one thousand kilometres from its eastern to its western extremities, more than half a million Ontarians claimed to be of Irish ethnic origin. In at least a quarter of the more than four hundred settled townships persons of Irish ethnic origin composed at least forty-five percent of the total population, and in about fifty townships they represented more than sixty percent of the population. The main areas of Irish settlement, (Figure 4.1) included cores in the eastern part of the province which had emerged as early as the first decade of the post-Napoleonic emigration, as well as the more recent concentrations in Grey County.[2] The social character of Artemesia Township and Markdale was an amalgam of English, Scots, and Irish settlers, some were pioneers who had helped clear the forests, others were merchants and craftsmen who had immigrated directly into the town. Significantly, every second person in Artemesia claimed to be Irish in 1871 and their presence was made all the more obvious by a clustering effect that had emerged early on in the settlement process. It has been observed that George Snider, the agent charged with overseeing the settlement of what would be Grey County, "had an antipathy against mixed nationalities. Therefore he placed different nationalities in separate settlements."[3] Coloured persons, who had been among the first to settle in the Queen's Bush were located along the old Durham Road, Catholic Irish were granted land in the vicinity of Irish lake and Scots were concentrated around Priceville. Elsewhere, although ubiquitous within the township by virtue of their numerical predominance, concentrations of Protestant Irish were also discernible.

It was hardly surprising therefore, that Benson was able to find many friends and neighbours among the ranks of his fellow Irishmen. Indeed, his story projects an understated Irishness in everything he did. He mentions Ireland at his critical life junctures and is wont to describe Irish people he remembers by their place of origin. In the Scottish phase of his adventures, his brother-in-law rented a house in Brigtown from a "man named James Smith, from County Derry". In Glasgow, he obtained goods for hawking from "Mr. John White, a Belfast merchant". He mentions the Irishness of a few others he encountered in Canada, such as the Dublin man O'Brien and "Dr. Dickson, a young surgeon recently from Londonderry". The communities in which he stayed and tried to settle were heavily Irish, or connected to the Irish immigration, whether in Brockville, Stuartsville,

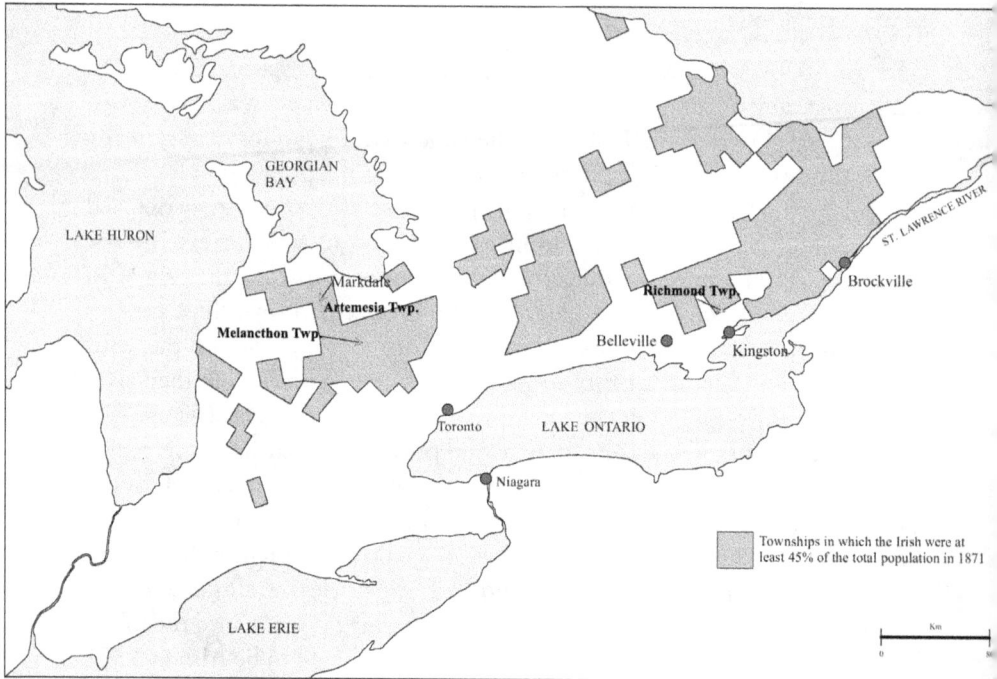

Fig. 4.1: Principal areas of Irish settlement in Ontario, 1871

Toronto, or Artemesia, because in each of these places the Irish immigrants had established a strong presence and added their culture to the colonial mix. This core of Irishness and an Irish immigrant world underpinned Wilson's Canadian world. By the time he settled in Artemesia he had sorted his friendships within an ethnic order. Most of the people he mentions in his life in Artemesia were Irish-born, married to Irish women, and had Canadian-born children, thus reflecting among the settlers a tendency to have spent time elsewhere in the colony before coming to Artemesia. Very few could be identified as newly arrived immigrants. Table 4.1 includes sixteen neighbours and acquaintances that Benson mentioned in his account of life in Artemesia. Among the sixteen men, all of whom have been identified in census and other manuscript sources, thirteen were Irish, two were English, and another an American. Their spouses also tended to be Irish but their children, in all but two cases, were born in Ontario. Benson's circle of acquaintances, like himself, had committed themselves and their children to the province. All but one of them was a farmer, the lone exception being Dr Mehaffey in whose home Wilson's second wife Agnes had worked before her marriage.

Table 4.1

WILSON BENSON'S IRISH FRIENDS AND NEIGHBOURS IN GREY COUNTY

Name	Place of Birth	Church
Christopher Irwin	Ireland	Wesleyan Methodist
Wife	Ireland	
Children	Ontario	
Alexander Madill	Ireland	Wesleyan Methodist
Wife	Ireland	
Children	Ontario	
Joshua Dodds	Ontario	Presbyterian
Wife	Ontario	
Mother-in-law	Ireland	
Thomas Kells	Ireland	Methodist
Wife	Ireland	
Children	Ontario	
John Mackay	Ireland	Presbyterian
Wife	Ireland	
Mr Lackey	Ireland	Church of England
Wife	Ireland	
Children	Ireland	
John May	Ireland	Church of England
Wife	Ireland	
Son	Ireland	
Dr Mahaffey	Ireland	Church of England
Wife	Ireland	
Children	Ontario	
Peter Rowe	Ireland	Church of England
Wife	Ireland	
Children	Ontario	
Thomas Gilbert	Ireland	Wesleyan Methodist
Wife	Ireland	
William Bowler	England	Wesleyan Methodist
Wife	Quebec	
Children	Quebec	
Edward Fagan	Ireland	Methodist
Wife	Ireland	
Children	Ontario	
Joseph Price	Ireland	Anglican
John Martin	England	Church of England
Wife	Ontario	
Children	Ontario	
R. Lever	Philadelphia, USA	Primitive Methodist
James Brady	Ireland	Church of England
Wife	Ireland	

Significantly the three principal Protestant churches – the Church of England, Methodist and Presbyterian – were all represented among the families and, just as significantly, the Catholic Church was absent. None of Wilson's acquaintances in Artemesia were Catholic. His is an Irish story and its cultural subtext is definitely Protestant and Ulster.

To our knowledge, his entire narrative, embracing his life in Ulster, Scotland and Canada, includes only one person who can be identified as Catholic – Michael McLaughlin, the miller at Mono Village (Mono Mills). In rural and small town Ontario where Irish Catholics accounted for less than one fifth of the population, the predominance of Protestants in Benson's world was to be expected but nonetheless the virtual absence of Catholics in his story is remarkable. Indeed the inclusion of McLaughlin in that story casts the miller in a less than flattering light. Around 1850 Benson had brought eight bushels of wheat to be ground for grist at McLaughlin's mill but while he was distracted someone stole the bags of grist. To explain the theft of his produce he surmised that fairies must have pursued the McLaughlins from Ireland and made off with his grain. He notes, rather ungenerously, McLaughlin's donation of "ninety pounds of very black flour" to make up for the stolen goods, and leaves us thinking that something else was amiss. He suggests that sitting at his loom in Ireland would not have presented him with such an unpleasant encounter. Unravelling the meaning of the anecdote that Benson weaves around the events involving the only known Catholic in his story presents an intriguing interpretive challenge.

Fig. 4.2: The site of McLaughlin's grain mill (Mono Mills)

The context of Benson's story, he being Protestant and from Armagh, would have been informed by the Irish traditions of William of Orange. He had grown up in the Orange heartland of Ireland, a few kilometres distant from the site of the 1795 Battle of the Diamond where the Orange Order was conceived. Orange culture and sectarian divisions permeated the roads and districts he walked as a youth. Likewise in Canada he traversed the colony's Orange heartlands where Protestant Irish emigrants had instituted the fraternal organization of their homeland, creating the largest concentration of Orange lodges of any country outside of Ireland. By 1899 there were more than seventy Orange lodges in Grey County organized into thirteen districts and they were affiliated with another one thousand lodges scattered throughout Ontario.[4] Markdale had, at times, two operating lodges and a fine Orange hall was constructed in 1885 by the Haslett brothers, owners of a large store and stove manufacturing factory and probably among the wealthiest men in the community.[5] The strength of the Orange Order in Markdale may be surmised from a report on the Twelfth of July celebrations of 1882 when it was noted: "At Markdale the Twelfth was signalled by a very quiet day indeed. Looking up the street in the afternoon not two people could be seen for tout le monde had gone to the grand picnic of the Orangemen at Mrs. Thompson's grove."[6]

From Brockville, founding place of the Canadian Orange Order, through Kingston and Toronto to Markdale Benson moved through communities that had strong and public Orange profiles. The ideology of Orangeism was stamped on Ontario. It became central to its strident sense of British imperial sentiment and it was supported by a complex hierarchical organization, an infrastructure of hundreds of Orange halls, and by the demographic preponderance of his fellow Irish Protestant countrymen. Wilson's own farm abutted an area bearing evocative transplanted names – Orange Valley and the Boyne River. Not far away Loyal Orange Lodge 1065 stood at the aptly named Protestant Corners. It was an Orange landscape as complex and as visible as any in the Ulster heartland.

The town of Markdale to which he migrated in 1874 had originated as a station on the Toronto, Grey and Bruce Railway and it also served as a market and service town for the neighbouring localities. The origin of the name Markdale reflected the influence of an emigrant from County Fermanagh, Mark Armstrong, who owned the property on which the railway station was built and who, like Wilson Benson, had been an early pioneer in the district. George and William Haskett, sons of Irish immigrants and local leaders of the Orange Order, were the most important local entrepreneurs and their hardware store and stove factory was a major employer of local men. Benson operated his grocery and general merchant

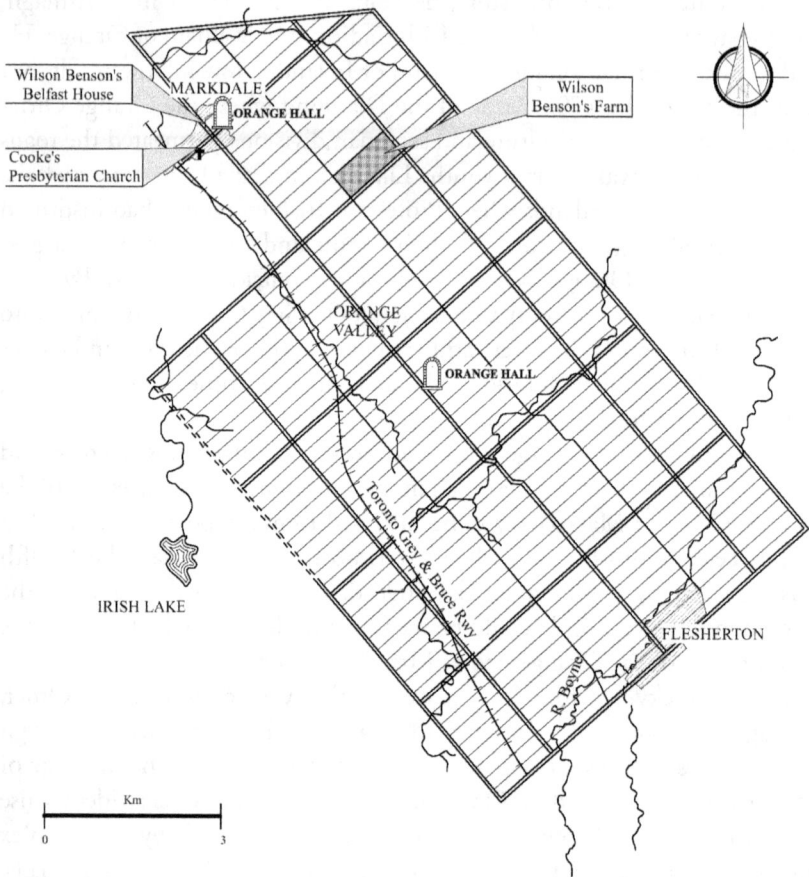

Fig. 4.3: Wilson Benson's environs, Artemesia Township and Markdale

business across the street from the Haskett store and as such was prominently located in the commercial core of the town. One of his main business rivals was Co. Tyrone immigrant, W.J. McFarland who was extensively engaged in the grain trade and owned a stave factory and a general grocery store.[7] In 1882 Cooke's Presbyterian Church was opened in Markdale and in its name it memorialised the Reverend Henry Cooke, a firebrand anti-Catholic orator in 1830s Belfast. The Markdale church had a contemporary in Toronto where Cooke's Presbyterian Church on Mutual Street was located within a few meters of the County Orange Hall. For several generations that church was regarded as a key supportive element in the Orange culture of a city that bore the appellation, "The Belfast of Canada."[8]

We do not have any evidence that Benson was himself an Orangeman as the documents needed to demonstrate his membership are no longer available. The only direct reference he makes in his narrative to Orange culture refers to an unfortunate sleigh accident that killed a friend on the main road by the Holland Orange Hall when Benson and his friends were en route to a political rally. We know that his children did participate in Orange entertainments in the Markdale Orange Hall and his son-in-law, J.S. Rowe, a music teacher in the local school, was an officer in LOL 1045 in the village.[9] We also know that the local doctor who attended the birth of Wilson and Agnes' daughter, Henrietta in 1870,[10] as well as Wilson after his accident at threshing, was the prominent Orangeman T.S. Sproule but we have no way to know whether Sproule's engagement with Wilson was solely medical.

Sproule was then building a political career through his leadership in the Grey County Orange Lodge. He had come to Markdale in 1869 where he opened both a medical practice and a drug and stationery store. He was a well-known, Ontario-born, Orange firebrand and popular speaker. From his base in Markdale he took a seat in the House of Commons, representing Grey East from 1878 to 1915 and attained considerable influence in politico-religious controversies arising from questions of imperial defence, the Jesuit Estates Bills, the Manitoba Schools Question, settlement in the West, and the status of the Papal Nuncio in Canada. He would serve as the Grand Master of the Grand Orange Lodge of British America from 1901 to 1911 and President of the Triennial Grand Orange Council of the World from 1906 to 1908. Markdale was Sproule's electoral base and a significant Orange centre. Benson, whether or not a registered Orangeman, was well placed to move within the local Orange ambiance even if his connection to Sproule was only happenstance because of the accident and the fact that the two men lived in the same town and in the same electoral district. Although they crossed paths and Benson's children probably attended the Methodist church that Sproule attended, we are not warranted to draw fraternal Orange links between them. That Benson lived, worked, and played among Irish Protestants is indisputable, but whether membership in the Loyal Orange Order was part of his life, and just another omission in his narrative, remains unknown.

Developing a Family Store in Markdale

Wilson suffered his accident at threshing on December 23, 1873 and just over a year later he and his family moved out of the house he had built and "opened a small store in the Village of Markdale, where I now reside".[11] During his convalescence he had sold his farm, bought and occupied a dwelling, stocked a store, and completed another major life-change. He readied his manuscript for publication and explained the complexities and personal impact of his accident, making clear that his buoyant self would not permit the "loss of my limbs" to drag him into despair. His autobiography ends at this point. He was fifty-five years of age and may well have felt that his life was nearing an end, yet he was determined to commence a new venture. His book gave the clear sense that he intended to continue in the community he had helped develop over the previous twenty-five years and to fulfil his family responsibilities. He and Agnes had six children at home, the oldest eleven years old and the youngest four, thus leaving him with their care for at least a decade. His responsibilities for Agnes could extend much longer. He lived for another 35 years with the determination and optimistic outlook he had always cultivated. Consequently, his published biography represents only three-fifths of his life span. The unwritten two-fifths of his life spent in Markdale are the subject of the remainder of this chapter.

In moving to the town, the Benson family relocated themselves within about two kilometres from their previous homestead and it is likely very few of Wilson's relationships would have been sundered. He and his two families could keep their social connections and circles of friends. The children of his first family were already independent. His eldest son, John, was married and working as a carriage maker in Markdale. Eliza Jane was also married and living nearby. Wilson Jr worked in the local wagon-making industry and married in April 1875. Jemima and Dorothy were in domestic service in Toronto, having married in 1874 and 1873, respectively.[12] His second family in their time would also move on from farming into urban occupations and professional roles. Many of the effects of the misfortunes from his farming accident were absorbed in the normal redirections of new generations to new opportunities.

Benson's decision to move to Markdale and develop a life based on retailing was both pragmatic and comforting. The family could not only stay among friends but also could pursue a livelihood with which Wilson had a long-standing familiarity. A subsequent occupant of the Benson farmstead, Mrs Blanche Quigley of Markdale, conveyed to the authors an oral tradition that confirmed him as an inveterate trader, selling wares from his own farmhouse during his time as a pioneer farmer[13] – an activity he did not reveal in his book. As a newly wed in 1943, Quigley had moved into Benson's former farmhouse and lived in it until it was demolished in 1960. The one-and-a-half storey house that Benson built in the 1850s to his own design had a simple rectangular plan, enclosing an unfinished attic the full length of the upper level and three finished rooms on the lower level. At one end of the lower level two small bedrooms were fitted side by side into the width of the house. The remainder of the lower floor, running two-thirds of the length of the house and in part over a root cellar, was one large working space serving several functions – kitchen, spinning and weaving room, a retail shop for the sale of goods to local farm families, and living room. Despite all the heavy work of clearing land and cultivating crops the Bensons retained their roles as shopkeepers. Wilson was well settled in Artemesia but he had not abandoned the survival techniques of trading and peddling acquired in his earliest working days. Quigley assessed Benson's house as being crudely built and insufficient, asserting that the two bedrooms were hardly adequate for a couple let alone a couple and several children.[14] And unlike the log houses occupied by his neighbours, Benson's dwelling was a timber frame structure clad with vertically hung planks that had no tongue and groove or comparable joining. Seasonal changes in humidity twisted and warped the planks on the frames and exposed cracks to let in winds and sometimes the snow. The Quigleys spent years fighting the elements that invaded the structure and Blanche told of waking one morning to find her husband apparently greatly aged, his whitened head encrusted by frost and snow. They replaced Benson's house with a new bungalow in 1960: the demolition of the old house revealing the secrets and shortcuts of a pioneer unskilled in building and cabinetry. Although the house may not have been an architectural gem, it had served as a home for a century for the Bensons, for the Mercers, then the Taylors and Shaws,[15] and finally the Quigleys. It had also helped familiarize Wilson's children with the retail trade.

Fig. 4.4: Wilson Benson's farm in Artemesia Township

COURTESY OF MRS BLANCHE QUIGLEY

Following his move to Markdale Wilson wasted no time opening a store he called the *Belfast House*. He purchased two adjoining premises on Mill Street North in which he maintained the store and where his family lived. The deliberate choice of the name *Belfast House* signalled the Ulster identity for a well-established immigrant clientele and implied a public house and availability of alcohol. Various whiskeys – Scotch, Irish and Canadian – and liquors of all kinds were major items among Wilson's stock but his start-up trade centred on groceries and the general provisions needed in town and country households – teas and sugar, tinned goods, flours, meat, and vegetables and fruits as available. He obtained goods both from local farms and from Toronto wholesalers via the railway, emulating a pattern of trade he had employed earlier on the steamers between Toronto and Kingston. He also appears to have brought fresh goods from the United States through travelling dealers of the Eastern Market in Detroit.[16] He publicized his low prices and used the retailing gimmicks of his time – discounts, giveaways, credit and catchy sloganeering, proclaiming: "I have no desire to puff or misrepresent the performance of impossibilities but I may as a response to a brother retailer who offers a book worth $1.25 to every purchaser of 3 lbs of tea that I will give Two Books of superior value to those mentioned to all buyers of a like quantity."[17] Indeed he

Fig. 4.5: Belfast House, Markdale

maintained a regular weekly patter of advertising in *The Markdale Standard.* He claimed to sell goods at the cheapest prices and promoted the arrivals of fresh goods to his stock. He presented an image of fair and honest dealing, and was not shy in his assertions. He claimed, for example, that: "As I do no puffing or blowing I want the Public to give me a call and be convinced what bargains I am giving, before you purchase elsewhere."[18]

Belfast House was a success, and by 1881 Benson had diversified the range of goods and expanded his trade. The town had benefited from the railway's arrival and the clustering of civil and commercial activities had given it a more significant service role than it would otherwise have had as an isolated rural village. Benson had also drawn three of his boys into the business, and at the ages then of seventeen, sixteen and fifteen they assumed additional responsibilities. At the end of March in 1881 he announced that "Those indebted to [me] would do well to settle at once and save further trouble as I am in need of money, being now engaged in the erection of a new brick building and require the money."[19] That building also signalled the advancement of his sons in the business.

As his boys became more experienced, Wilson ceded management to them and slowly eased himself out in time for the *Belfast House* to become the *Belfast Block* in 1889. The three boys, James, Thomas, and Robert, were then in charge and we may speculate that they engaged in some property transfers to consolidate and finalize family issues. In 1888 Robert and James acquired from their half-brother John two town lots in Markdale amounting to a fifth of an acre on Mill Street South. John was closing his carriage building enterprise in town and moving to Toronto. He had acquired the lots in 1874 just before his father sold the farm and we surmise that the

Business Jealousy

Just because it is our good luck to do a great deal more business than our share, our competitors then they begin to squeal. This is one way of getting satisfaction:

March 16, '94.

Dear Sirs :

Mr. W. J McFarland requests us to enquire by what authority you occupy his lot adjoining your store premises. We are instructed to say that unless you AT ONCE remove the wood you have had placed on said lot, and pay the sum of two dollars for the use of the same, proceedings will be taken against you without further notice. We are

Yours truly,

Lucas & Wright.

To Messrs. R. H. & W. J. Benson, Markdale.

We had 3¾ cords of wood piled on said lot for about five weeks. Owner of above said lot used our delivery cart on and off for about five years, and we paid the Blacksmith for repairing!

We are to the front this spring with the finest stock of Dry Goods, Groceries, Boots & Shoes, Ready-made Clothing, Hats, Crockery & Glassware. The highest price paid for all kinds of farm produce. Bring along your Butter and Eggs. You'll make money by buying from us.

R. H. BENSON & CO.

Fig. 4.6: Wilson Benson's marketing rivalry with W.J. McFarland, *The Markdale Standard*, February 15, 1894

transaction in 1888 may have had an origin in the earliest days of their father's decision to move to Markdale. Between the purchase of the lots by John in October 1874 and their disposal to James and Robert in August 1888 the property was used by each of John and his three merchant half-brothers to float mortgages to fund unknown activities. We may speculate that Benson may have wanted to support John's advancement through the purchase in 1874 but, in exchange, kept a silent interest in ownership and final disposal of the property.

Whatever the motives behind the property transfers, the brothers had shifted their basic retail business toward general merchandise and dry goods. They continued to sell groceries including local eggs, butter and meat but they also increasingly targeted a younger and female clientele influenced by urban fashion trends in clothing, shoes, boots and furs. They also stocked Irish linen, something that, no doubt, pleased Wilson, the old handloom weaver. The youngest son Robert became the leading voice in the enterprise and with his brothers Thomas and James *Belfast House* was redeveloped and branded as R.H. Benson & Co. They continued Wilson's approach to a weekly advertisement in *The Markdale Standard* and were opportunistic in highlighting the failings of their business rivals, particularly W.J. McFarland with whom they shared a mutual animosity. Wilson continued his work in the store and Agnes withdrew to their house on Main Street.

The Second Generation

R.H. Benson & Co. appears to have flourished under Robert's general leadership until the early years of the twentieth century. The firm was responsive to changing consumer tastes, adjusting its goods and sustaining a good reputation while attempting to extend its market from the Markdale base. From the early 1890s and through economic recessions in Ontario and slow growth in the West, the Bensons opened stands and outlets in other towns. We cannot date any of the moves precisely but we have established that they operated satellite stores in Dundalk, Shelburne, Owen Sound, Copper Cliff, perhaps Sudbury, and Indian Head, Saskatchewan. James apparently left Markdale about 1894[20] to undertake management of the operation at Shelburne, about fifty kilometres from Markdale. Over the next decade he would manage (at one time or another) the R.H. Benson & Co. outlets in Dundalk, Owen Sound and Indian Head.[21] Thomas served the firm in Dundalk, Owen Sound and Copper Cliff. Robert remained at Markdale, overseeing the whole operation. The three brothers were known for "their characteristic industry and sticktoitiveness, with geniality"[22] and the firm appears to have done relatively well for the brothers personally. No

Benson's,

Belfast House

Noted for keeping a first-class article and selling at the lowest possible living prices. Our great clearing sale of

OVERCOATS, OVERCOATS, FUR CAPES, MUFFS,

— AND —

Winter Underwear

is still going on. Have only a few lines left. We have no traveller's samples that have been peddled all over the country and handled by every Tom, Dick and Harry for sale. No rat eaten woollen goods for sale. We keep in stock nothing but the very best of goods. We have too much respect for our customers to offer them anything but a first-class article.

SALMON TROUT,   ❋

    WHITE FISH,

        FRESH WATER HERRING,

    ❋   SALT WATER HERRING,

BONLESS CODFISH,   ❋

        ORANGES, LEMONS,

    ❋   DATES, FIGS,

—— HEADQUARTERS FOR——

Wines, Liquors, Ales and Cigars,

R. H. BENSON & CO.

Fig. 4.7: *The Markdale Standard*, March 16, 1894

record of the company has been located but some clues appeared in social notices. In preparation for his wedding in 1898 Robert built a substantial house. The local newspaper commended its owner and builders:

> There's not a more complete, comfortable and convenient residence in town than that of Mr R H Benson which has just been completed. It is situated on Wellington Street, built of brick with

69

stone foundation, heated by furnace, has bath room, hot and cold water, and is lighted by electricity. It is a model of good taste and convenience from cellar to garret and the workmanship is certainly creditable to the mechanics, viz. stone and brick, C Fox; plastering Joseph Gibson; carpenter, W G Richards; plumbing, D A Ward and painting by J J Cherry. Mr. Benson and bride are now up the lakes on their wedding trip.[23]

Robert and his wife were prominent members of Markdale society and they featured regularly in the local *Markdale Standard*. His brother James also received some attention and on his wedding day in 1905, the newspaper reported that the groom presented the bride with a cheque for $500. No evidence of Thomas' relative prosperity has been identified. Despite the public display of apparent success, events in 1903 and 1904 showed that the firm was struggling. Their business strategies were insufficient to sustain operations and in April of 1904 the Bensons announced that the home store in Markdale would close.

R.H. Benson & Co. was undoubtedly encountering difficulties but the manner in which the brothers responded via advertisements in *The Markdale Standard* conveyed a strong impression that the brothers were simply moving to a better location and stronger market in Owen Sound. They wound up the Markdale business in a very positive way. In early 1903 the firm announced that it was adding wallpaper, carpeting, paints and other home decoration products to its usual range of goods, a signal of confidence or perhaps of significant competition drawing away clientele. Later in November they announced the closing of their Dundalk store and the start of a three-month sale of stock there. From this point the process unfolded in quick order and we may wonder how much of it was carefully planned to dispose of their stock and real estate without having the business appear to have failed. The stock remaindered from the Dundalk sale was shipped to Markdale to create *"A DOUBLE STOCK—Two Stores in One"* bargain sale announced there on March 3. The advertisements focused on business as usual and for three weeks the sale proceeded until March 24 when they announced the "biggest Cut-Knife Slaughter Sale ever given in this country" because the Markdale store had just been bought by Mr James Kelly, owner of the Revere Hotel in town. The firm's general manager, James Benson, had also returned from the West for a temporary two-month stint to dispose of the stock. In front page news on April 14 the local newspaper informed the community that the R.H. Benson & Co. would close its Markdale store in three months and that James Benson would leave "for the west on a business and prospecting trip shortly but as to future arrangements for locating [the business] we cannot yet speak definitely".

Out of public view, the Bensons were considering other options. On May 5 they advertised that tenders were wanted for the "erection of a new brick block in the village of Dundalk", the town they had just left. An interest in the West may have been suggested in August as Robert and James placed on the market 10,000 acres of farmland on the prairies. In September the "slaughter sale" that began in April was extended until the end of the year and all customer accounts were to be settled by the first day of January. Any remaining debts were to be turned over to a local law firm. In the background the brothers were negotiating with Meir & Co. of Owen Sound for the purchase of the "Arcade". They opened their new business there in Meir's former premises in October and closed the Markdale operations at the end of December. *The Markdale Standard* reported in January 1905 that:

> After doing a successful business first as a grocer and later in the general mercantile line, the Benson Brothers have located in Owen Sound. They have been among our most progressive business men, and for close application to business and taste and order in and about their store they would be hard to excel … We regret to lose them as business men and neighbours, but they have the best wishes of this community for continued success.

The brothers decided neither to rebuild their business in Dundalk, nor go to the West, but to stay close to home. Their decision recognized a slightly larger and growing market in Owen Sound. What roles, if any, Wilson and Agnes played in the decision is not known.

The firm's response to its changing market position is understandable when seen in the context of the structural changes then underway in retailing. The Benson's competition came first from businesses in Grey County and other towns along the railway link to Toronto as economic changes consolidated the locational advantages of some towns. Roads too had been improved for the new automobiles and the effects of distance were much reduced, thus presenting the people of the region with new options to go farther for higher value goods. They were drawn away too by the appeal of an urban culture whose appeal had rapidly spread into rural communities and turned the preferences of the pioneers' children toward city styles. All these factors had an impact on the Bensons' business but their first apparent response of adding wall, floor and window coverings to decorate the houses of a more settled rural community did not meet the primary challenge they faced. It did not remove the profit constraints of sales on credit, the heavy costs arising from unpaid accounts, and the burden of unsold inventory. Many other retailers faced similar issues but successful solutions required new operational methods and a greatly expanded scale of business that the Bensons may not have been able to initiate in Markdale.

In the 1870s, the innovation of mail-order retailing had been adopted in the United States to deal with the very issues that beset the Benson's operation. By taking advantage of the spreading network of railways to deliver goods speedily and efficiently to rural areas, mail-order firms could offer lower prices and higher quality than could local merchants. Toronto's T. Eaton company, following from the success of American pioneers, started its catalogue operations in 1884 and was aggressive in meeting the requirements of the younger customers for variety, guaranteed quality, and an inventory of new products. How the Benson brothers interpreted the consumer dynamics is impossible to say but they stayed with the model of personal service for customers and goods available on local credit for as long as they could. Eventually they realised the impossibility of maintaining a network of stores in half a dozen small urban centres. Owen Sound appeared to be the best choice for a more centralized operation. Personal factors may have also influenced their decisions. For example, soon after closing the Markdale store, Robert moved more than two hundred kilometres to a store in St George, his wife's hometown in Brant County. His father-in-law moved in with the family. Thomas may have gone with him.[24] There may also have been concerns about the eventual care of their elderly parents, Wilson and Agnes. In that regard, James continued as manager of the Benson business in Owen Sound until he retired to Toronto about 1911 or 1912[25] a date that followed shortly after the death of Wilson, and may finally have brought to an end the commercial connections between the Benson brothers and their father's legacy.

The rest of the progeny of Wilson – Jemima and Agnes, made their way into the new economies and places of North America and all have stories worth being told. The example of their father in publishing a personal sketch was not taken up but each of them had the material on which to build such a biography, at least for the interest of their nearest and dearest. The lives of the daughters unfolded in diverse ways. Jemima's surviving daughters married and established families. Elizabeth Jane, born in 1845, married Joseph Irwin from the Artemesia area and lived in Markdale for most of her life. Sarah Ann, born 1848, married James Galbraith from Markdale and appears to have had a comfortable life. Jemima, born 1853, and Dorothy, born 1856, both moved to Toronto, perhaps together, Jemima marrying Henry Popham and Dorothy, Frederick Songer. Popham was a saddler and Songer a coachman. In the Wilson and Agnes marriage, three girls were born and survived. The eldest, Mary Ella, born 1868, trained as a dressmaker, moved to Pennsylvania and later studied nursing.

She married a Dr Eastman, spending much of her life in Pittsburgh, but eventually retiring to Los Angeles where her husband was a distinguished member of the medical profession. Henrietta, born 1869, was a music teacher and married James Rowe, the Markdale school headmaster. In 1912 Henrietta left Markdale and rejoined her husband who had already moved to Brantford. She had cared for her father in his last days and the coincidence of her leaving Markdale after his death parallels James' retirement from the Benson business; their departure from the town reflecting the termination of the strong familial bonds that had existed between Wilson, Agnes, and their children. The youngest daughter, Isabella, born in 1871 and the namesake of Isabella who died of infantile cholera in 1860, moved to Cleveland and became a nurse, marrying Jacob Worbs, secretary-treasurer of an electrical manufacturing firm and a wealthy member of Cleveland society.

On the male side of the families, the two men of the first family, John, born 1843, and Wilson Jr, born 1849, were mechanics in the carriage and wagon making trades. Although both started married lives in the vicinity of Markdale, they settled with their families in Toronto. John married Annie Ireton from Glenelg, a township adjoining Artemesia and Wilson Jr married Hettie Page from Owen Sound. Wilson Jr also worked twenty years or so as a shopkeeper selling cigars and then about a dozen years in confectionary. The three men of the second family were the merchant brothers who built upon their father's life in retailing. Robert, born 1866, married Nellie Cooper and eventually moved to her hometown of St George, in Brant County, and continued there as a merchant. James, born 1864, married Agnes Henry from Owen Sound and they eventually retired to a house in Toronto on High Park Boulevard. Thomas, born 1865, spent some time with Robert in St George and the last part of his life in Los Angeles. We do not have Thomas' marital records but he appears to have remained unmarried. All the children seem to have maintained connections of some kind with Markdale and followed each other's whereabouts, especially during the life of Agnes and Wilson.

At the funerals of Agnes and Wilson, the children memorialized their parents whose impact on their lives had been very great. With the exception of Robert who was ill, all of Agnes' children attended her funeral in 1908. Her obituary carried the family's sentiments. It read:

> After a protracted illness, borne with Christian patience and fortitude, Mrs. Wilson Benson breathed her last on Monday, the 25th [of May]. Coming to this community many years ago, she and her husband were among the early pioneers of this neighbourhood, and witnessed the forest-covered land develop into cultivated farms.

She was a member of the English Church, and in the family circle the influence of a good mother was always felt. As a loving mother, she was devoted to her children, and always welcomed them in their visits during her declining years … Many and beautiful were the floral offerings banked around the casket, their perfume reminding one that mother Benson's life was beautiful and the memory of it is indeed sweet.[26]

Three years later Wilson died. The cause of death was recorded as "senile dementia." *The Markdale Standard* acknowledged the children who had come to the funeral from other places, John and Wilson Jr from Toronto, Robert and Thomas from St George, and Isabella from Cleveland. His obituary said nothing about his role as a father or husband, but focussed instead on the strength of his nature, and recalled his life in the simplest manner:

Mr. Wilson Benson, one of the early pioneers of this district, and who had almost reached 90 years of age, passed away on Sunday, the 18th of June. Deceased was a man of remarkable vitality, his intellect continuing clear almost to the end. He was a native of Belfast, Ireland, but a resident of this district these sixty years, thirty-five of them in Markdale. Interment took place at Markdale Cemetery on Tuesday p.m. the 20th, Rev. E. G. Dymond officiating at the house and the grave.

Fig. 4.8: Benson family gravestone, Markdale

In the last piece of his business, his will, Wilson acknowledged all of his children except the two girls Jemima and Dorothy who had settled in Toronto. The three sons of Agnes received the lions' share of the proceeds.

In June 1957 the last two surviving Benson children, Mary Ella aged eighty-nine from Los Angeles, and Isabella aged eighty-six from

Cleveland, travelled for the last time to Artemesia and Markdale to visit the places of their childhood. Their eighty-eight-year-old sister, Henrietta, remained behind at home in Los Angeles. In Markdale, Mary Ella and Isabella visited the hospital and made a donation of $3,000 that is commemorated by a plaque in the hospital foyer dedicated to "The family of Wilson Benson".

Notes and References

1 Benson, 129.
2 A fuller description of the settlement patterns of the Irish in Ontario is contained in Cecil J. Houston and William J. Smyth, *Irish Emigration and Canadian Settlement, Patterns, Links and Letters* (Toronto and Belfast: University of Toronto Press and Ulster Historical Foundation, 1990).
3 Grey County Historical Society (ed.), *Markdale and Flesherton: A Written Heritage* (Markdale: 1979).
4 Address by E.F. Clarke to Orangemen gathered in Owen Sound, July 12, 1899, *The Sentinel*, July 13, 1899.
5 Mildred Young (ed.), *Markdale, The Crossroads of Grey* (Markdale: 1988), 25.
6 *The Markdale Standard*, July 13, 1882.
7 *Markdale, The Crossroads*, 5.
8 William J. Smyth, *Toronto, The Belfast of Canada: The Orange Order and The Shaping of Municipal Culture* (Toronto: University of Toronto Press, 2015).
9 *The Markdale Standard*, December 29, 1904.
10 In May 1930, Robert Benson registered the birth of Henrietta with Ontario authorities. He named T.S. Sproule as the attending doctor. Robert's document was provided on the Page Family Tree of Ancestry.ca. According to the Weselyan Methodist Baptismal Register in the Toronto Reference Library (M592) Henrietta was born on April 10, 1869, not on May 4, 1871 as proposed by Robert Benson.
11 His move probably occurred on February 1, 1875. The first of ten annual installments on the mortgage was scheduled for February 1, 1876, thereby suggesting February 1, 1875 as Mr Mercer's first day of possession and Wilson's date of exit. G.S. 2194 #1345 (Archives of Ontario).
12 Henrietta (Dorithy) married in Toronto, October 3, 1873 and Jemima married in Toronto on April 16, 1874. Both women are absent from the 1871 census for Grey County and Toronto. Both retained contact with their family in Markdale. In 1897 Jemima spent two weeks with her father (*The Markdale Standard*, October 14, 1897) Dorithy's daughter, Effie, kept house for James and Thomas Benson in Markdale in 1903 and her sister, Birdie, was a flower girl at the wedding of her half-sister, Ella Benson, in 1903. (*The Markdale Standard*, September 10, 1903.)
13 Information provided by Mrs Blanche Quigley, Markdale, June 1991.
14 Ibid.
15 *The Markdale Standard*, February 2, 1905 reported the Mercer's sale of the Benson farm to Alf Taylor for $5,000.

16 This is an interpretation of Wilson's statement. The only use of "eastern market" arises in US sources. Detroit and Washington, DC are the two sites of historic Eastern Markets. Detroit was connected with Canada's Grand Trunk Railway via Port Huron – Sarnia.

17 *The Markdale Standard*, October 15, 1880.

18 Ibid.

19 *The Markdale Standard*, March 25, 1881.

20 Revealed in his obituary in *The Markdale Standard*, June 29, 1925.

21 Ibid.

22 *The Markdale Standard*, April 14, 1904.

23 *The Markdale Standard*, July 14, 1898

24 Thomas was reported as living in St George in *The Markdale Standard*'s report of his father's funeral, June 28, 1911.

25 *The Markdale Standard* reported in the obituary for William Benson, June 29, 1925, that he had retired about 1912. As no other member of the Benson family was engaged with the store at that time, we have assumed that was the end although we do have virtually no information on the company's affairs after the move to Owen Sound in 1904.

26 *The Markdale Standard*, June 4, 1908.

Conclusion

The story of Wilson Benson's life in Ireland, Scotland and Canada is not a heroic tale of improbable achievement, attainment of a manifest destiny and accumulation of vast riches; neither is it a tale of failure and regret lived out among strangers in an alien environment separated from the land of his birth by an ocean and half a continent of partially settled land. It is an ordinary tale of coping with adversity, of commitment to a path of modest improvement and the attainment of acceptance within a new society that was maturing at a pace commensurate with his personal experience. He had emigrated from an Ireland that was located on the cusp of great economic change and tottering towards the human tragedy of the Great Famine that would kill one million people and push another million onto emigrant ships within a decade of his departure. In an experience common to hundreds of thousands of his fellow countrymen Benson and his very young wife crowded onto a converted cargo ship that had been temporarily fitted out with bunks in the communal steerage; risking their lives and possessions in a voyage that was certainly perilous, lengthy, and uncomfortable in the extreme. It was a brave decision but it was not without precedent among his friends, relatives and neighbours in contemporary mid-Ulster. Mass migration was a phenomenon of the place and the era.

The scale of population relocation at local, regional and global levels altered dramatically in the early nineteenth century. A revolution in transportation, world trade and political circumstances created conditions in which rapidly industrializing cities and settlement of the remaining temperate grasslands and forested areas of the mid-latitudes would generate a frenzy of migration; providing space and opportunity for the burgeoning number of Europeans who participated in transoceanic migration in the century 1815–1914. Emigrants from the British Isles contributed 22.6 million to that migration flow and within it the Irish numbered about seven million. At the time Ireland was home to about one percent of the population of Europe yet it contributed fifteen percent of the international migration and for eight decades in the century before the First World War Ireland was ranked first among European countries in terms of the annual average rate of emigration per 1,000 population.[1]

For a time in the 1820s and 1830s the Canadian colonies outstripped the United States as a route to a new life and even in the darkening days of the 1840s the lure of the remaining British territories in North America remained strong. Native peoples and French settlers had staked earlier claim to the region but in the maritime colonies of New Brunswick, Nova Scotia and Prince Edward Island and further west in of what now constitutes Quebec and Ontario, there remained vast tracts of unsettled land – forested but with good agricultural potential. It was in these lands that the foundations were laid for the Second British Empire, largely coterminous with the 'long nineteenth century', 1783–1914. In large measure the new colonies helped compensate for the loss of the American colonies in the closing quarter of the eighteenth century. Canada emerged to become the favourite colony of the new imperial political entity. By the eve of the First World War, Britain and its empire were home to almost 400 million people and its territorial extent embraced about one-quarter of the global land mass. No other polity on earth could equal the extent of this enormous demographic and geographical power and within it Canada loomed large; displayed on Mercator world maps by a solid red band wrapped around half of the northern hemisphere.

Within that empire the complexities of politics, trade and economic organization bound the Canadian colonies to a powerful metropolitan core in Britain. The maintenance, and indeed intensification, of imperial connections was sustained by movement of people, ideas and cultures from the heartlands of Britain and Ireland to the colonial frontiers, and onwards within the new settlement regions.[2] In that respect the developing Canadian colonies represented more of an imperial outpost rather than a colonial outback and, notwithstanding an initial simplification of cultural complexities, the course of subsequent adaptation to the new homelands bore the unmistakable imprint of enduring connections with the old. In that respect, Wilson and Jemima Benson found both a daunting newness and a reassuring familiarity when they sought to establish themselves as Canadians. Everywhere they travelled they encountered fellow Irish folk. The rhythms of small-town life, farming and peddling haberdashery and whiskey were familiar as were the social infrastructure of schools, churches and Orange lodges. Those recognizable ambiances resonated in Brockville and Kingston where they spent their initial years and in Toronto they would have encountered one of the most Irish of all North American cities. In the "Queen's Bush" they certainly encountered a different ecology of flora and fauna, and the climatic regime of the continental interior was more extreme than the temperate environment of Ireland, but even there the seasonal rhythms of frontier farming, and bouts of peddling haberdashery and whiskey recalled much that was familiar from their earlier lives. The friendship of fellow pioneers and the support of an emergent community eased the process of social integration and fostered a growing identification with things Canadian.

The pioneers did not create their new agricultural landscapes in a vacuum. They worked within a prescriptive system that had determined, in most cases, the boundaries of farm lots and township administrative units prior to the allocation of occupancy rights. Bureaucrats decided the names of the township units in advance and little heed was paid to local input. But yet the settlers did find ways of reconstructing their cultural identity in the alien landscape and the veneer of official nomenclature was supplemented by more familiar place name insertions such as Irish Lake, Protestant Corners, Orange Valley and Boyne River all of which identified communities and localities proximate to the Benson homestead. The very scale of the Irish influx ensured that there was sufficient mass to support cherished aspects of culture. In 1825, for example, some 20,000 Irish crossed the Atlantic and annual levels of migration in the 1830s reached 60,000 per annum. More than half of them were destined for Canada, with Ontario receiving the majority of that latter group. The first Canadian census (1871) after Confederation recorded 850,000 persons of Irish descent, one quarter of the national population: more than half a million of them lived in Ontario.

It was in this milieu that Benson established for himself a life that was undoubtedly more rewarding than that which he might have expected had he remained in Ulster. But he did not do it alone. Jemima was a mainstay for twenty years and apart from tending the house and rearing a family she performed additional tasks that contributed greatly to the financial well being of the family. Her skills as a dressmaker and willingness to perform menial housework tasks generated an income in the weeks and months immediately after their arrival in Brockville when Wilson was demonstrably incapable of securing a regular income. Over the next few years while her husband operated a seasonal regime on the lake boats Jemima continued as a homemaker, and she also minded a grocery store and bought goods that he could trade among the lakeshore communities. She was sufficiently brave and worldly-minded that while Benson remained on the lake boats she willingly embarked, in the company of her brother, on a reconnaissance of potential settlement lands in 1849, bringing along a barrel of whiskey to trade on the frontier during the trip. Benson found it difficult to cope without her and after her unexpected death in 1861 he confessed to being "gloomy and spiritless" for some time.[3] He remarried a little over a year later and the shortness of the period since Jemima's death probably reflected not only the need to have a woman to look after his young family but also denoted the importance of family units on the settlement frontier. The demands of land clearance, house construction and farming required labour inputs greater than what could be readily provided by one individual. In Canada the supply and cost of labour represented an inversion of that which prevailed in contemporary Ireland. In the latter country labour was plentiful and cheap; in Canada it was scarce and expensive. The assistance of his growing children and a wife were critical to the overall success of what was in essence a family enterprise. Census records reveal that the Bensons produced considerable amounts of wool and cloth in their Artemesia farm house, and that too would have required from all in the household some assistance in treating the wool, spinning and weaving.[4] Furthermore, local lore indicates that Benson continued to maintain a supply of merchandise, including whiskey, for sale to his neighbours while he was farming in the township and that too would have required the help and cooperation of Agnes who would have minded the store in the same way as Jemima had twenty years earlier in Richmond Township.

Jemima is an essential figure in Benson's autobiography, mentioned occasionally and only partially rendered. His second wife, Agnes, receives even less attention in the narrative but both were important to Wilson's life and legacy. Their contributions were not only monetary and familial: as women on the frontier they were also a central mainstay in a process that saw an orderly society emerge from a raw beginning. Benson describes in some detail the savagery of inter-county brawls among the male encampments of Irish canal workers and in contradistinction he portrays a settled scene in Richmond Township where he "erected a snug house, although in the beginning of winter, and opened a grocery, which my wife attended, while I travelled through the country with a miscellaneous stock of wares."[5] It is this sense of family completeness and implicit rootedness that renders improbable an interpretation of the narrator's life as being an embodiment of transiency. In Armagh he could return to the home of his father whenever he wished. While tramping through the lowlands of Scotland for six months in the 1830s he had the company of his sister and brother-in-law and depended upon them. In Canada his wife and family were rooted in a home environment while he plied his trade as a peddler and operated in a seasonal capacity on the lake boats. In Canada, as in Ireland, he maintained reference points to which he could, and did, return.

There was nothing haphazard about his life or the places to which it took him. He operated according to the dictum that "God helps those who help themselves" and conducted his life moderated by the advice of others and protected by the love and support of two wives and twelve children. The support of his family remained central until the end of his life. In 1901, by which time he had handed control of his store to his sons, he and Agnes lived in the centre of Markdale next door to his daughter, Henrietta and her husband James. Three houses away there resided the proprietor of the Bensons' business – his son, Robert and family. A few months before Wilson's death in the summer of 1911 the census noted that Henrietta and her daughter were living with him, caring for him in his terminal dementia.[6] Henrietta's husband had moved to Brant County and on Wilson's death Henrietta would rejoin him. The grave marker in the local cemetery did more than recall the lives of Wilson, his two wives and an infant daughter: it signified the final resting place of a man who had spent sixty years in the immediate vicinity and who, according to the local paper, was a native of Belfast and a man of considerable vitality and intellect.[7]

Notes and References

1   Stephen Constantine, 'Migrants and Settlers', 163–87 in Judith M. Brown and Wm Roger Louis (eds), "The Twentieth Century", *The Oxford History of the British Empire vol. iv,* (Oxford: Oxford University Press, 1999).
      For a wide-ranging discussion of the new approach to imperial history see Judith M. Brown and Wm Roger Louis (eds), *The Oxford History.* Also Andrew Porter (ed.), *Oxford History of the British Empire,* vol. iii (Oxford: Oxford University Press, 1999).
2   Philip Buckner, "Whatever Happened to the British Empire", *Journal of Canadian Historical Association,* 1993, 55–85, presents a challenging interpretation of Canadian colonial relations.
3   Benson, 130.
4   Grey County agricultural census, 1871.
5   Benson, 112.
6   1901 and 1911 manuscript censuses, Grey County.
7   *The Markdale Standard,* June 28 1911.

Index

LIFE AND ADVENTURES

OF

WILSON BENSON.

WRITTEN BY HIMSELF.

"Multum in parvo."
"The Divine right of Kings is co-existent with the Author of Nature."

TORONTO:
HUNTER, ROSE & CO., PRINTERS, WELLINGTON STREET WEST,
1876.

The publication of the History of my Life, Travels and Incidents relating thereto will be shortly put in press, and trust it may be found sufficiently interesting to merit a place on the shelves of every family library in the land, and solicit the good wishes of all in the promotion of my venture.

WILSON BENSON.

We the undersigned Ministers of the Gospel beg to recommend the above work to the kind notice of the public.

Rev. J. W. ROBINSON.
Rev. J. A. McALMON.

DEDICATED TO

His Excellency Lord Dufferin, K.C.B.,

GOVERNOR GENERAL OF THE DOMINION OF CANADA,

Commander of the Forces, &c.,

IN TOKEN OF HIS EMINENT SERVICES IN THE CAUSE

OF LITERATURE AND ART,

BY

The Author.

PREFACE.

THE author presents this little volume to the public, hoping that the perusal of its pages may afford amusement where it does not otherwise interest; that, in reading the ups and downs of life incident to myself, others may be nerved when beset with apparently insurmountable difficulties; and to the student of nature it may serve to guide him clear of shoals upon which I have ran aground. A review of my past life convinces me of the necessity of a well-matured, well-directed course of action laid down in youth for the guidance of our future lives, combined with an unwavering purpose in execution; it is the only true road to prosperity and social greatness.

In publishing this volume, I have no ambitious end to serve; my humble aim has been to preserve, from oblivion and the ashes of the past, a sketch which might serve future generations in the compilation of a future History of Western Canada (Ontario). When the first portion of this work was written, it was not intended it should ever be printed; but the solicitation of friends, whose opinions prevailed, induced me to revise what 1 had written, and add such additional items of interest as might conduce to the information and amusement of the general reader.

Looking upon the history of one's country as an heir-loom, to be preserved at all hazards, has been the chief incentive to my taking up my pen, in my humble way, in that behalf. The fruits of perseverance, the results arising from energy and enterprise in the prosecution of our daily business, is one motive I have endeavoured to inculcate in the substance of the following pages.

BIOGRAPHY.

THE writer was born in the City of Belfast, Ireland, in the month of December, 1821, where my father kept a weaving shop, employing a number of men. When I was about a year old my mother died, and was buried in the family burying-ground in Drumcree Churchyard, near Portadown.

Soon afterwards my father relinquished business, and removed to the Townland of Drumnasue, near Portadown, where he contracted a second marriage with a widow lady who was about being ejected from her small farm for non-payment of arrears of rent. He paid the demand, built a new house on the premises, and made other improvements, and all went smoothly on for a period of ten years, when the sons of my step-mother by her first marriage obtained possession of the premises through neglect of my father not obtaining a transfer of the lease in his own name, and he received a mere nominal sum for his outlay in improvements. Being thus suddenly reduced to penury, I was, in consequence, compelled, at twelve years of age, to hire with a man named Wm. Cullen, receiving a salary of 4s. 6d. sterling for three months' service. I then engaged with a reedmaker named Wm. Hyde, receiving 6s. 6d. per quarter, and remained three years, although my labour was hard and treatment worse.

About this time I returned to my father's, where I received a few months' schooling, being nearly all the day-school I ever attended. At that period the National School system of Ireland had not been fully extended over the country as it now is; hence those whose means were limited found it difficult to obtain an ordinary Common School education, the absence of which in my own case has frequently been a bar to my advancement in life.

At this period a married sister, who had been living in Scotland, paid us a visit, and through her influence I resolved to try my fortune in "the Land o' Cakes," and accompanied her home, with the sum of 12s. 6d. stg. in my pocket. We left my father's residence in the Townland of Mullantine, and journeyed through Belfast and Newton-ards to Donaghadee, where we were delayed setting sail till Sunday morning by reason of a storm; but when out a short distance the storm returned with increased violence, and what with the foaming and hissing sound of a tempestuous sea, and the firing of distress guns, the impression made upon my mind on that occasion can never be effaced. Arrived at Portpatrick, on the Scottish coast, in the night, drenched with spray and rain—wet, cold, and hungry—and after a long and diligent search found house-room to sit in till morning, without refreshment, the reader may readily conceive the state of my feelings on this my first trip on the journey of life.

On the following day we left by the way of the Glens of Glenope, Wigtonshire, our destination being Maybole, where my sister's family resided. The country was

mountainous and but sparsely settled, except by numerous
bands of gipsies, who were met at short intervals, having
huts burrowed out in the sides of the mountain, busily
engaged in the manufacture of tinware. Numerous
herds of black cattle and sheep browsed in every direction. A distance of some thirty-five miles brought us to
Stranraer, and in that vicinity I for the first time in my
life saw a veritable snake. Being possessed of the usual
accompaniment of a travelling Irishman—a sturdy blackthorn stick—and having heard in my time that the *touch*
of Irish blackthorn would instantly kill a snake, I tried
the experiment, but found it required *force* added to the
touch before the reptile was killed, which proved to be a
black adder about three feet in length. The upheaval of
the earth in many places caused me to examine the cause,
and I ascertained that it was the work of moles—or
mudies, as they are termed in the native dialect—which
are unknown in Ireland.

Our journey brought us to "the banks of the clear
winding Ayr," where we saw Burns' monument, and spent
some two hours in the vicinity. The scene was impressive; the landscape was dressed in Nature's loveliest garb
—the broom, thistle and whin were all in full bloom—
and whether the sense experienced arises from reverence
of Nature's noblemen, or that the spot possesses hallowed
charms, the visitor is impressed with a desire to linger
and dream of the past. A peculiarity I observed in the
river Ayr was a curl or ruffle on its surface, even in the
most sheltered places, where not a breath of wind disturbed
it. We stayed two days in the town of Ayr with a rela-

tive, and for the first time saw " bang-the-beggars," dressed with coats having red collars and cuffs, and whose duty was to arrest mendicants and alms-seekers.

The next town of importance on the route was Falkirk, where may be seen the monuments of Wallace and Knox—the former noted for his doughty deeds of war, and the latter no less remarkable for his tenacity of purpose in the cause of his religion. The place wore an air of antiquity which led me to conclude that modern go-ahead ideas of progress had not penetrated there.

On arriving at Maybole, we found brother-in-law sick and in the hospital, and after a few days' delay we all left the place, *en route* for Glasgow. Our funds being low, we were refused lodgings, and for three successive nights slept at hay-stacks. On the fourth night, being refused admission at a farm-house, we took shelter in the sheep-house. Many of the ewes were suckling their lambs, and whether or not in accordance with the strict law of *meum* and *tuum*, we deprived the lambs of a share of their mothers' milk, which we drank with a relish. Let it not be considered by these remarks that the Scotch are an uncharitable people—for did space permit, numberless acts of benevolence to us might be here recorded ; and their extreme caution in entertaining strangers may have arisen from previous travellers " playing sharp," thus rendering their proverbially cautious natures doubly so.

Little worthy of note occurred till we reached Kilmarnock, where I first saw the Kilmarnock night-cap. The country was hilly, yet thrift and prosperity abounded on every side. Dairying is carried on extensively throughout this district, and the tons weight of cheese to be seen at each farm-house would appear incredible to those who have never seen the manufacture of this article conducted on a large scale.

We reached Glasgow in due time, and my brother-in-law soon found employment at his profession as a weaver, in the Calton suburb. We resided in Brigtown, near Hussey's cotton mill—I believe one of the largest in Scotland at that time. My brother-in-law rented a house from a man named James Smith, from Co. Derry, Ireland. I found occupation in the cotton mill as a piecer, but soon gave that up, and, with eighteen pence in my pocket, made my way to the wholesale house of Mr. John White, a Belfast merchant, doing business below the Salt Market, Glasgow. He trusted me with another eighteen pence worth of miscellaneous goods. In the first week I cleared eight shillings, and continued the business for twenty-one weeks, placing my earnings each week in the hands of a weaver named Robert Young. My route led me to Paisley, Ruglin Brig, Busby, and was prosperous. I attended Glasgow Fair, which lasts six days, and the variety of character congregated there would furnish an excellent field for the observation of the physiognomist, and scope for the efforts of the philanthropist and humanitarian.

About this time my brother-in-law signified his intention of going to the Lothians, and I resolved to accompany him, and called upon my banker Young; but when I asked him for my deposit, he put me off with the remark that he would have it for me on my return.

We started for Edinburgh, our route taking us through

the town of Airdrie, ten miles distant from Glasgow, and to which point the railroad had just been completed. The road was lined with a motley crowd of Irishmen and women, Highlandmen and women, all bent in the direction of the Lothians for the harvest; but as the harvest was not likely to commence for two weeks, and the distance only forty-two miles, they only averaged about five miles per day, using all manner of subterfuges to obtain food. In some cases a man would be raised upon a comrade's shoulder, when he would march into a wealthy farm-house, lay the fellow on the floor, and notify the inmates that the man was dying of hunger, that they were too much exhausted to carry him further, and that he (the farmer) might bury him. This generally had the desired effect—provisions in abundance. On another occasion a cadaverous-looking Celt was deposited with a more than ordinary wealthy gentleman. The fellow assumed to be at the last gasp, and upon the gentleman remonstrating, he was coolly informed that they had done even more than their duty, for it was very probable they had already caught the infection of yellow fever from him. This last was effectual; for they not only received all the provisions and beer they could consume, but a handsome sum of money likewise, to carry the fellow away and bury him. On one occasion an Irishman and a Highlander had a set-to at fisticuffs, and when tired of knuckles, resorted to their reaping-hooks, and by a " turn of the wrist " the Irishman got a slash in upon his opponent, slicing down the greater portion of the left hip. Fights between the two branches of the Celtic family were of daily occurrence, as they understood each other sufficiently to give vent to their mutual hatred.

Immediately on my arrival in Edinburgh I procured a small stock of fancy articles, which brought me some profit, my route taking me to the summer resort of plea-sure-seekers at Portobello, and occasionally to Mussel-boro'. The picturesque scenery around Portobello, with its elegant cottages, in every imaginable style of architec-ture, makes it one of the most charming towns I ever visited. On one occasion a dead sea-horse was driven ashore in a storm, the inhabitants eating the flesh. It was about the size of an ordinary three-year-old colt. Cockles are more abundant here than at any other place I ever visited.*

When harvest commenced, I engaged with a gentleman named Hope, about one mile from Portobello, my duty being to assist a boy and girl making porridge for some three hundred hands employed in the harvest, the gentle-man cultivating upwards of one thousand acres of land in various kinds of grain, besides stock raising on a large scale. The porridge pot was larger than an ordinary potash kettle, built into an arch, the potstick being moved by horse-power—one person guiding the "stick," while another poured in the meal. The porridge was taken to the field in large tubs, on carts, the average weight being about sixty hundred weight for a breakfast

---

* Edinburgh is certainly a magnificent place, whether we view it in the architectural grandeur of the New Town, or the stately majesty of the Old Town. High Street is very appropriately named, as the houses in many instances are fourteen stories in height. St. Mary's Wynd is one mile long, and is principally occupied by pawnbrokers. Castle Roe is an imposing edifice, and lends an air of stately magnificence to the city.

meal, each gang of six reapers receiving a quantity equal to about a small wash tub, and a "chappin" of four quarts of butter-milk. Dinner was composed of a two-penny "bap" and three half-pints of ale to each shearer. All hands returned to the house for supper, which was composed of porridge and milk in the same proportions as for breakfast, except that the three hundred shearers were seated on the grass in a circle, the laird and lady, with other visitors, looking on the while in evident glee at the "happy family" scene before them—Irish and Highland working with a will to fill a depleted stomach. The beds were loose straw, spread in two parallel rows the length of the barn, with a small space between, a blanket and quilt being allowed to each three who were companions on the "rig," all being thus huddled together promiscuously, regardless of sex. After remaining three weeks, the harvest being then over, I started on Sunday morning for Glasgow, and after three days' fruitless plead-ing with banker Young, I embarked on board the steamer *Arab,* for Belfast, where I landed with just one shilling in my pocket, sixpence of which I gave for a ride on the railway cars to Lisburn, making the remainder of my way home on foot, a distance of twenty-three Irish miles. The first acquaintance I came to was my former em-ployer, Wm. Hyde: he was glad to see me. I again engaged service with him, at former wages, and remained there some six months. I then went to live with a man named James Ford, Townland of Cruebeg, near Pointz-pass, in the Co. Armagh, and remained three months. Here we tried the experiment of killing fleas. The peat stack was near the house, and year after year's accumulation of peat mould had created a bed for the hatching of the little pests. A comrade named Thomas Hall frequently chewed tobacco at night, and I observed that where the juice fell on the floor, numbers of dead fleas might be seen in the morning. This gave an idea to my mind, and we tried the experiment of fumigating the bed clothes and house with vapour of tobacco and brimstone. This effectually rid the house of those pestiferous backbiters.

At the end of six months I returned to my father's, and remained about two months, when I apprenticed myself to a man named William Courtney, Townland of Bottle Hill, Parish of Kilmore, for a period of four years, to learn the linen-weaving business; my remuneration to be a guinea a year and a new shirt. Before the half of my term had expired, my master confessed his inability to teach me anything of the art : however, I remained until within three months of the expiration of my term. Small as was my remuneration, I could not obtain a shilling, and had to appeal to my father for clothing. About this time a *charivari* commenced in Bottle Hill, which at one time caused me some uneasiness. The wedding party were surrounded with an uproarious assemblage, carrying bundles of burning straw and throwing it among the processionists. Finally, three or four policemen appeared on the scene, but they were immediately knocked down and their muskets taken from them. Reinforcements came, and we (I was among the number) were compelled to take safety in flight, running in rear of Lady Richardson's demesne; thence to the Armagh road and home. A few days afterwards several arrests were made, and I was in constant dread of apprehension. Being engaged in the harvest-field reaping, a comrade raised the false alarm that the police were coming, which so startled me that I cut myself severely on the left hand. During my residence there I laboured very hard, frequently far into the night. I attended a night school at Bottle Hill school-house, which gave me a knowledge of writing. I also attended a Sabbath school for two years, which also contributed to my small stock of learning. I left Mr. Courtney and went back to my father to Mullantine. I commenced weaving on my own account. Shortly afterwards the "Big Wind" came, in the fall of 1838—a hurricane which will be long remembered by every resident of the British Isles at that period. The roof was taken off my father's house, and falling rafters, beams and *debris* smashed every thread in a linen web I had recently put in the loom. I set to work and took up the broken threads, ripped out a piece of the damaged cloth, put it into the reed again, and although it was a 22-hundred fineness, I completed my web; and on presenting my work to Mr. Dunbar, linen draper, Banbridge, for whom I was working, he gave me a premium of half a guinea, as no such task had ever before been undertaken. I took the weaving of several webs from Mr. William Bennett, Potash Mills, near Tandragee. On one occasion he wished several webs of linen woven in a given time, to complete a shipping order he had received, and offered premiums of 10s., 5s. and 2s. 6d. to those who would bring in their webs first in the order named. The webs were all of equal fineness, measuring fifty-two yards each. I was one of the competitors, and on the fifth day after receiving the yarn I returned the web, being two days in advance of any one. I never slept, in the real sense of the word, during that time, except an occasional "nod" while working at the loom, and a web of the same fineness is considered good work in three weeks.

My father removed from Mullantine to the Townland of Bottle Hill, in the Parish of Kilmore, where I continued my occupation of weaving. At this time I made the acquaintance of a young lady named Miss Jemima Hewitt, who attended the same Sabbath school as myself. She had learned the dressmaking profession in Rich Hill. Our acquaintance soon ripened into a closer relationship than friendship, and we were married privately, our extreme youth—I was eighteen years and she sixteen years of age—rendering us doubtful if our respective parents would give consent to our union on that account. But, on the fact becoming known to them, they one and all heartily acquiesced in our little *ruse*. I remained with my father during that winter, and resolved to try America in the spring.

The customary preparations for an Atlantic voyage were soon made; leave-taking—messages from friends in Ireland to friends in Canada. A voyage across the Atlantic in those days involved many discomforts and privations totally unknown in these days of rapid steam navigation. Seven, eight, nine, and as high as thirteen weeks were not unfrequently occupied by sailing vessels on the voyage; and the consequent suffering experienced on such occasions, the news of which, when transmitted by the sufferers to relatives at home, had spread an universal dread of a trip to America, and I must confess that I was not without my misgivings; but the incentive to brave the danger was caused by my desire to achieve a home and independence in the Western World which the force of circumstances denied me in the land of my birth.

Myself and wife took passage in the ship *Sarah Stewart*, of Belfast (Captain Lowe), bound for Quebec. We cleared on the 28th March, 1841, and had a pleasant voyage for four days, when a storm arose, and during the next three days we every moment expected to go to the bottom. A sum of five hundred sovereigns was raised amongst the passengers and offered to the captain if he would return to Belfast, but he declared that he dare not do so for any consideration, although we were up to the knees in water on the lower deck. The terrors of that period of three days cannot be described by pen of mine; it must be experienced to be fully appreciated.

When three weeks out, disease made its appearance, and eight children and one man fell victims to its ravages. I had frequently heard of sharks following ships which contained a corpse, and attributed the remark to superstition; but certainly, whether by accident or otherwise, a shark followed us during two days previous to the burial in a watery grave of the man just mentioned, and was seen no more by us. About this time we experienced a dead calm, which continued for three days.

When on the Banks of Newfoundland a dense fog prevailed, which I believe is customary in that part of the ocean, owing to the meeting of the warm waters of the Gulf Stream with the colder waters of the North Atlantic, and still more rarefied by the numerous icebergs met with in that quarter, eleven of which we saw at one time, requiring great caution in the night to avoid collision. One night during the fog, and while a stiff breeze was blowing, the watch on the bow discovered a large vessel bearing right down upon us, and only a few yards distant. The opposite vessel appeared to have discovered us about the same time, for the bows of the two vessels barely grazed each other, and, with the loss of a piece of bulwark and spar, no further damage was done.

While on the Banks we fell in with a vessel in distress, keeping before the wind by means of a jury-mast, her rigging and masts having been swept away in the same storm which we experienced on the 3rd and 4th of April. She was on a voyage from Mexico to St. Helena when the disaster befel her. They hoisted signals of distress, and our vessel hove-to, when they sent a small boat alongside, and we learned that they were entirely destitute of provisions and water ; and out of a crew of nineteen, only five—the captain, second mate, cook, and two seamen—remained. They were plentifully supplied with provisions by the passengers, our captain also supplying them with whatever was necessary to take them on their voyage to Liverpool, whither they signified their intention of proceeding. A rumour had gained currency in British ports that the *Sarah Stewart* was lost, and all hands drowned; but the arrival in Liverpool of the disabled ship mentioned dispelled these illusions, much to the joy of our friends at home.

Captain Lowe was a strict disciplinarian, but his general demeanour both to seamen and passengers was brutal in the extreme ; indeed, on some occasions he seemed to be partially insane, for in a frenzy one day he took the ship's carpenter into the hold of the vessel, with auger and axe, to scuttle the ship. The vessel was lost on her return voyage, but the crew were saved, and the captain died of brain fever afterwards.

With the exception of a storm in the Gulf of St. Lawrence, there was not much worthy of note on the trip up the river, the beauties of which have been so frequently described by abler pens than mine. The grandeur of its natural scenery, and picturesque beauty of the many charming villages which stud its banks, and the glittering tin roofs of the houses, in the effulgent rays of an April sun, forms a panorama not readily forgotten. Arrived at quarantine, we passed the same day, on our way to Montreal, where I arrived with two sovereigns in my pocket. From thence we took barges for Kingston, being towed up the river by oxen and horses. On two occasions, in ascending the rapids, the current was dragging the boat and teams out into the river, when the drivers were compelled to cut the hawser with an axe. It occupied ten days between Montreal and Brockville. There was a delay here of an hour before the steamer that was to take us in tow to Kingston, and myself and wife went into the town, but before we got back the boat had left. I followed next day, and found the chest containing my luggage in the boat, but it had been broken open, and the most valuable portion of my own and my wife's clothing, bed clothes, &c., were stolen. I returned to Brockville next day with my chest, and concluded to reside there. My wife hired out to do general house work. However, times were so bad I could not find a stroke of work to do, neither in the town nor the country round about. My money was exhausted, and the first night in Brockville I took lodging in a tolerably respectable looking tavern; but after getting to bed, the fleas and bed-bugs appeared to be at war which of them should take possession of me. This was my first experience of bed-bugs, and the torture was so great that I arose, dressed myself, and went out into the street. I wandered on to the burying-ground, and laid down under a pine tree, where I slept soundly. Such was my first night's experience in Brockville, which I continued nine nights in succession.

I went out to the " Tin Cap," some miles from Brockville, but not finding employment, and being too proud to beg, I slept at night in the fence corner. I returned to town dispirited and gloomy, as the times were not only bad, but the prospect ahead was far from reassuring. The country was not yet settled into business working since the disturbance of Mackenzie's rebellion, and no part of Canada had felt its effects more severely than in the neighbourhood of Brockville and Prescott. Although the rebellion scarcely deserved the name, in its insignificance, compared with that which was opposed to it, yet it carried with it a significance which was not to be misunderstood. The negotiations for the union of Upper and Lower Canada had prevented the authorities from entering upon any public works; this, no doubt, tended to increase the general stagnation in business.

Shortly after my return I received employment from a gentleman named Manhardt, living about three miles from Brockville, at weaving a web of full-cloth. Woollen goods were entirely new to me, being differently arranged in the loom, and a hand-shuttle. However, I accomplished my task, producing a fabric which my employer pronounced superior to anything of the kind ever before woven for him. This was the first work I obtained in Canada. I next engaged with a man named Phillips to work on his farm. He asked me if I could plough, which I, in my eagerness to obtain employment, answered in the affirmative, trusting to luck as to how I should succeed; for be it known I never guided a plough in my life, except once in Ireland I held a plough after a rude fashion down one side of a field. The first two or three days I was occupied in general duties, which gave no reason to my employer to complain. The morning arrived, however, when we were to commence the dreaded ordeal of the plough. Whether the old gentleman had doubts of my ability in that branch of duty I know not, but he again asked me if I could hold a plough, when I promptly answered, "Yes, on the barn-floor." He replied by telling me it was in the field he desired the holding done, when I assured him that I had been raised on a farm, and followed it all my life. Arrived at the field, I attempted to start the team down the furrow, when the horses took fright, probably at my bad management, and using the " prrruuushshsh " instead of " whoa " and ran away ;

and although they did not get loose from me, they dragged
me round and round the field. I managed to prevent
them getting over the fence, which they seemed much in-
clined to do. The proprietor was in the field, and assisted in getting the horses pacified; and just at that moment a tremendous thunder shower providentially came
up, which prevented any further attempt at ploughing
for the next three or four days. My time was occupied
during the remainder of my time here in weeding carrots
and other vegetables. Owing to a disagreement, my
month's term of agreement came to a termination in about
seven days, and with seventy-five cents' remuneration for
my services, I started for Brockville. Phillips was blind of
an eye, and his good wife had a pair of reel feet, which
rendered them a remarkable pair.

Soon after my arrival I engaged with a man named
Lusher, a hotel-keeper, of Yankee origin, to act as porter,
attend the arrival of the steamers, &c. On one occasion,
when on my duties, taking luggage off the steamer bound
to Ogdensburg, the boat moved out into the river before
I was aware of it, and I was unwillingly taken to that
place, and compelled to wait till the next day before another boat came along, bound to Brockville. Lusher's
house had been the head-quarters of a volunteer troop of
Canadian horse during the rebellion of 1837–38, but
owing to information having been learned that he had
been in secret communication with the rebels, he was never
paid a farthing of the debts incurred. It was a standing
joke in Brockville for many years afterwards that "the
British sucked in Old Lusher."

I then engaged with a Scotchman named James Nicholson, to learn the baking and confectionery business. At this time I was located so that I saw my wife every day; for to the outside world we passed as brother and sister, without producing the evils which a similar *ruse* on the part of Abram and Sarah of old brought upon the House of Egypt. My time here was spent very pleasantly, and I soon acquired a good practical knowledge of the art of making my own bread, by making bread for others. The thought of returning to Ireland, however, I had never abandoned, and my only desire was to acquire a trade which would serve me better there than weaving. Experience taught me that a journeyman baker was not that profession, and after a stay of six months I abandoned the business.

I next engaged with a Dublin man, named O'Brien, to learn shoemaking; but a two days' apprenticeship convinced me that "lasts" and "pegs" and "wax ends" would not last me in pegging out an existence to the end of my days.

In 1842 I engaged with Mr. Geo. Chaffey, of Brockville, who carried on an extensive agricultural implement manufactory, employing a great number of hands, and he was, without exception, one of the most gentlemanly employers I met, either before or since. The times were dull, and his manufactory suffered in consequence, and in the fall of the year he commenced discharging his employees. He called me into his office one day, and informed me of his determination to reduce his expenses, but that if I was unemployed in the spring he would then give me employment. I asked him why he discharged *me*, "for," said I, "it takes very little work to keep me going." He burst into a hearty laugh, and gave me employment till spring. I would here mention, that from the time I engaged with Mr. Chaffey, my wife and I had kept house on our own account. My wages were $14 per month and board myself, and my wife found constant employment at her profession of dressmaking; so that we lived comfortably and saved money.

In the spring of 1843 Mr. Chaffey paid me in full, and said that as he was going to Toronto, I had better accompany him, as I intended going West; but while on our passage on the steamer *Brockville*, I engaged as cook on board the vessel, at $10 per month. Having no immediate use for the money I had in my possession, amounting to $60 or $70, I returned it to Mr. Chaffey for safe keeping, without any other security than his word of honour.

Our route was principally between Kingston and Dickenson's Landing, and the varied scenery on that part of the Thousand Islands was delightful in the extreme. The commander, Capt. Maxwell, was an excellent officer, of genial manner, and this rendered my position more pleasant. My knowledge of paste and pastry, learned in Brockville, came in good stead in my new capacity of cook, and I had here ample opportunity of developing any latent power I might possess in the culinary art. I taxed my energies in the performance of my duty to the utmost, and believe I was rewarded with that degree of success which always attends well-applied, persistent effort.

The fall was now approaching, and as the steamer was about to "lay up" for the winter at Kingston, and as I had the promise of a continuance of my services upon her next season, I resolved to move my wife to that city. Accordingly, on the last trip down the river, I got off at Brockville, packed up my household goods, and not only received my money from Mr. Chaffey, but percentage for every day he held it in his possession. This was an act of generosity I could scarcely have expected.

Arrived at Kingston, I rented a house on lot 24, Stewartsville, Kingston, where I opened a small store, stocked it with groceries and other miscellaneous articles suited to the trade of the locality, and was tolerably successful. My experience during the winter of 1843-44 was uneventful, and presented nothing beyond the usual routine of life, except that on the 21st of November a great snow storm came on, and as I was returning from town with a tin stove on my back, on crossing the commons, I fell into the vats of an old tannery which had never been filled up, except by snow, and was nearly smothered before I could extricate myself.

In the spring of 1844 I recommenced my duties on the steamer *Brockville*. The only route of travel between the West and Montreal was by the St. Lawrence steamers· and it furnished me frequent opportunities of becoming acquainted with the persons of many of the leading men of that day, many of whom have passed to their long home. Politics were at that time carried on in the most violent partizan spirit, the zeal of the different advocates leading them to such an excess of ardour that the merits or demerits of their respective causes were lost sight of in personal praise or abuse of the party leaders they severally worshipped. These occasional episodes in my steamboat life not only amused me, but furnished food for reflection, and awakened in me a new and lively interest in the country, and begat a feeling of identity in its welfare which supplanted the yearning desire I had hitherto entertained of returning to my native land.

The Cornwall and Beauharnois Canals were under course of construction at this period. A riot occurred on the latter work between the Cork and Connaught Irishmen. The former, being the most numerous, obtained the mastery. News of this reached the Cornwall works; the Connaught men here, who were most numerous, determined to avenge the cause of their party, and drove the handles out of their picks, and with other bludgeons fell upon the Cork men with an energy which would have done credit to a better cause. The steamer was lying at the wharf at Dickenson's Landing at the time, and some of the fugitives took refuge on the boat. The assailants attempted to follow, when a fierce hand-to-hand conflict took place, the boat's crew taking part to prevent their (the assailants') entry. Two men had their brains beaten out in sight of the boat, the wives and children of the murdered men rending the air with their piercing shrieks while the bloody butchery was being enacted. The repeated onslaughts upon the boat compelled us to move out into the stream; and for a length of time afterwards a body of volunteers was compelled to keep guard to prevent the infuriated mob from carrying into execution the threat that they would burn or sink the *Brockville*, on such nights as we lay there. Peace was only restored by the withdrawal of the Cork men from the works. The same spirit was manifested on the Brantford Canal, which was in course of construction at that time, but with less disastrous results. My countrymen earned for themselves an unenviable notoriety, and produced an impression, especially among the rural population of Canada at that time, that the Irish, one and all, were "hard cases."

During the winter of 1844–45, Captain Maxwell purchased a large quantity of oysters and fresh haddock, which he employed me to peddle through the neighbourhood of Kingston. On one occasion, while passing through the Indian woods between Napanee and Belleville, I found the mail-bag belonging to the main route between Montreal and Toronto. It was shortly after nightfall, and the bag was so heavy that it was with much difficulty I lifted it into my waggon, taking it to Belleville, and delivered it to the Stage Agent there. Shortly afterwards, Captain Twohy, of the mail line, gave me ten dollars as a reward for my honesty. The contents of the bag were valuable, as it contained the money for the quarterly pay of the several garrisons of troops then in the West.

In 1845 I continued sailing in my former capacity, but my eyes, which had shown threatening symptoms the previous season, now became so much inflamed that I was compelled to abandon the business, and in a short time had to be led by the hand through the streets. I had the services of Drs. Samson and Robertson and others, but experienced no benefit. One day a gentleman accosted me respecting my ailment. His name was Dr. Dickson, a young surgeon recently from Londonderry, Ireland. Ascertaining from me that I had been acquainted with his uncle in Portadown, also an eminent surgeon, he invited me to accompany him to his surgery, where he operated upon my eyes, and in three weeks they were entirely well, and have remained so ever since.

In 1846 I shipped on the *Britannia*, Captain Maxwell, formerly of the *Brockville*, running from Kingston down the St. Lawrence to Montreal, around by the Lake of Two Mountains, and the Ottawa River to Bytown (now Ottawa), thence by the Rideau Canal to Kingston. During the season we had numbers of emigrants from the Old Country, many of whom were in a destitute condition and dying of fever. On several trips we have had two and three deaths between Montreal and Kingston. On one occasion, as we were entering the first lock on the Rideau Canal at Bytown, a little Irish girl, about eleven years of age, had just received a quantity of tea from me which she was carrying in a vessel, when the boat gave a lurch as the girl reached the deck, and she fell overboard and was drowned. After considerable delay the body was recovered, and Captain Maxwell, to his credit be it said, would not allow the boat to proceed on her voyage until the afternoon of the following day, when the child was buried.

During this year I was on other boats. While on the *Grenville*, Captain Smith, who kept a tavern at Kingston, because I would not play cards and spend my money as did the other hands on the boat, I was discharged. I then shipped on the *Traveller*, owned by Hooker & Henderson, Captain Taylor, running principally on Lake Ontario. Times being bad, and traffic scarce, the owners determined to lay the boat up, and consequently she was placed on the "ways" for repairs. I was employed as watchman on her for two months, which ended my boating for that season. I then bought a horse and waggon, and went to peddling through the country around Kingston.

I had a brother-in-law living in the Township of Richmond, some thirty-five miles from Kingston, and owing to his representations I removed there, purchased an acre of land, and erected a snug house, although in the beginning of winter, and opened a general grocery, which my wife attended, while I travelled through the country with a miscellaneous stock of wares. Money was out of the question, and trade in the shape of black maple sugar, hogs' lard, plucked poultry and bad butter—the former and latter realizing less in Kingston market than I paid for it. One circumstance in this connection I wish specially to mention :—I attended Kingston market twice a week, and travelled all night on such occasions to be on hand early in the morning. The beast I drove was a noble animal, named Sally, and when her name was mentioned shot ahead like an arrow. On one of my journeys to Kingston, having a female friend in company, one tollgate on the way was half open, and I at once conceived the mischievous idea of "running the gate." Accordingly, when within thirty or forty yards I shouted to the mare, and we flew past just as the toll-keeper hailed us to stop. I replied that the mare was running away, and I could not hold her ; but when some thirty rods past the gate, my companion's bonnet flew off, and I drew up and went back to recover it, when the toll-keeper in drawers and stocking-feet came up at the top of his speed, and I had barely time on returning to the sleigh to jump in and shout to the mare, leaving the poor toll-keeper just as he was about to place his hand on the sleigh.

In the spring of the year the sheriff made a seizure upon the property of the man from whom I had purchased my acre of land, and as I had not obtained a deed, it was included in the sale. I had expended a considerable sum in the erection of the house, and as I ascertained there was no redress, I accepted an offer of a cow valued at seventeen dollars for my improvements. This was a stunning blow to the future prospects I had pictured to myself ; but

" What is the use of repining ? "

So I set to work and made my calculations that as I already possessed one cow, I would purchase another, and that with the milk of those and my own earnings, we might do better in Kingston. One debtor in the neighbourhood owed me a load of straw and two sheep ; these I sold for three dollars, and with my little effects I retraced my steps to Kingston.

Arrived in Kingston, I again rented a house in Stewartsville from Mr. Edward Noble, and opened a store in connection with my small dairy and was doing tolerably well. Soon after a neighbour's cow broke into my stable, and gored one of my cows, so that she died in three weeks afterwards. I sold the other cow for $10, and thus again was my stock in trade reduced to a low ebb. I began to realize the truth of the proverb that "three removes are as bad as a fire"—equal to a total loss. I had been industriously engaged for five years climbing the ladder of fortune, and here I was at the lowermost rung.

On the opening of navigation (1847), I shipped on the boat *St. Thomas*, as cook, the route being around Lake Ontario. The boat was leaky—so much so that myself and the engineer left her at Port Dalhousie. The captain would pay us nothing, as our month was not up. I went back to Kingston, and worked around town for a time, and finally removed to Toronto, where I opened a small store of miscellaneous goods on Victoria Street. The difference in price of vegetables and fruit in Toronto compared with Kingston caused me to open up a trade between the two places. I stood the Kingston market while my wife purchased in Toronto, and forwarded to me by boat. The rot had become so bad that a cask of potatoes shipped at Toronto on Saturday in apparently sound condition, were totally rotten when opened in Kingston on Monday following; but on the whole I had no reason to complain of success.

In 1848 I engaged on the steamer *William the Fourth*, belonging to Cook & Calvin—Captain Day, of Ogdensburg. Our first trip was to the "Head of the Trent," to Prescott. Our next trip was to Port Dalhousie, to tow a large raft of twenty-one drams belonging to Mr. Marsh, of Port Hope. The boat was also laden with fifty cords of wood. When between Port Hope and Oswego a storm sprang up, and what with the tremendous load and the increased power given the engines to keep the raft up in the storm, she " broke her back," to use a nautical phrase. The planks started from their places, and the water spouted in through the opening with a hissing sound, striking the upper deck. We were thirty miles from the nearest land, and it was only a question of time how long the vessel would float. All hands were called into consultation, when Mr. Marsh at once proposed to abandon the raft and save the men ; but how to reach the Frenchmen on the raft was a question more easily proposed than solved. However, Mr. Miller, of Prescott, first mate, was equal to the emergency. He asked me if I had any hams in the pantry, and I replied I had large Chicago hams, when he ordered me to peel off the rind and bring them to him. A number of quilts and blankets were procured, and after much labour these were crushed into the opening with handspikes, and coal tar sprinkled thereon ; then the rind of the hams was securely nailed over that, and more coal tar applied, which effectually stopped the leak, and the vessel carried us safely to our destination at Garden Island. Without waiting for repairs we proceeded to Prescott. One man aboard was ill of fever and ague, and I gave him a bottle of my ague cure, which cured him in less than two days. I might here mention that I had been subject to attacks of ague during the first three years of my boating life, and, singular to relate, the means of cure were revealed to me in a dream. The man to whom I have just referred was mate of the vessel, and he was so

3

weak that he fell down while at his post at the wheel. I gave him the usual dose of a wine-glassful of the mixture, when he fell down apparently as if dead. I had the presence of mind to administer a few spoonsful of melted butter, which caused vomiting, otherwise it is questionable if he would have recovered. The dose was too strong for his debilitated constitution.

On the return trip to Kingston, a man and his wife were passengers. The captain forcibly landed the man at Firman's Wharf, and took the woman on. The man took the land route, and the following day arrived in Kingston, when he had Capt. Day, the first mate, and engineer arrested. The captain was fined a trifling sum, and thus the matter ended. We left Kingston to take another raft in tow without making any repairs, and the only precaution taken to secure our lives in case of similar peril to that which threatened us on our previous voyage, was the acquisition of an open scow, and, not thinking this safe, I left, and engaged on the steamer *Transit*, Capt. Richardson, running from Toronto to Niagara and Queenston. I continued on this boat during the remainder of the summer. My wife continued keeping store on Victoria Street, Toronto, and our several earnings placed us in comfortable circumstances for the coming winter. A part of this summer I spent in travelling through the Niagara district and the West, selling my ague cure, and circulating advertisements. I cured hundreds of cases in the peninsula, and many in Toronto can testify to its efficacy.

In 1849 I shipped on the schooner *Rose of Milton*,

Capt. Hamilton, cruising on Lakes Ontario and Erie. On one trip to the town of Erie, Pennsylvania, for a cargo of coal, while lying at the dock, a diminutive negro man, with a white beard, came on board the vessel, and inquired of me if this was a British vessel. On being informed that it was, he desired to be secreted, stating that he was a runaway slave, and that his pursuers were on his track. I at once secreted him in a closet which served as a store-room for vegetables, &c., and as we were almost ready to set sail, I did not discover his presence to either captain or crew until we were some distance out on the lake. When he appeared, Capt. Hamilton inquired of me where I had obtained " that child," and on being informed, expressed some anxiety, as we were liable to be captured had we been followed by a steamer. As it was, he merely looked up at the rigging, and exclaimed, "Blow, breezes, blow!" The negro, who knew no other name than "Sambo," we brought to Toronto. On one occasion, when I offered him some molasses, he shook his head and made grimaces expressive of disgust. He informed me that the slaves employed on the sugar plantations, when beaten by their masters, in order to obtain an indirect revenge, spat in the syrup, and committed other filthy things as an imaginary punishment upon the whites. I frequently saw Sambo in Toronto, and many times he expressed thankfulness to me for his deliverance I may here mention that shortly after the arrival of Sambo on board the *Rose of Milton* at Erie, two suspicious-looking men, dressed in plain clothes, came aboard and paced up and down the deck several times, and as all the crew were absent at the time, I felt some apprehension for the safety of the poor fugitive; but seeing nothing of a suspicious appearance, and the almost entire absence of the crew, they sauntered away. I made several other trips up and down the lakes during that summer on the same vessel.

In the fall of that year we loaded with flour at Gamble's Mills, on the Humber, for a last trip, bound to Kingston, where we loaded with salt as a return cargo. When off "The Ducks" on our return trip, we were overtaken by a storm, and with much difficulty succeeded in running into Presqu'Isle, where we were compelled to remain three days, on each of which we attempted to put to sea, and were as frequently compelled to return. This was on the 2nd, 3rd and 4th of December. The intense cold froze the spray, which constantly lashed over the vessel, as soon as it fell. The deck I liberally strewed with salt, which kept the water from freezing. The ropes and sails were unmanageable. On the fourth day, the wind having somewhat abated, we put to sea, and succeeded in reaching Port Hope the same day. Next morning we set sail, and in twenty-four hours afterwards we anchored in Toronto Bay. As soon as we landed, I resolved to abandon sailing, and have religiously kept my resolution ever since. During the summer I took my eldest son on an excursion trip to Kingston, and when near Toronto, on our return, I observed a fire in the city, and the impression instantly forced itself upon my mind that it was my house on Victoria Street; and to my consternation, upon my arrival the premonition proved too true, for I found my goods and household furniture on the street, much of which was lost beyond recovery, and a barrel of beer, which had been rolled out, by some means got the tap turned, and the contents ran away in a stream down the gutter of the street.

Immediately after quitting the schooner, a brother-in-law of mine, who lived in the immediate vicinity of Orangeville, came to see me, and from his representations of the benefits of farming, I sent my wife up with him to ascertain from her how she liked the place. I sent a barrel of whiskey with him to sell for me. Soon after this I received a letter informing me of the death of my father, in Ireland, which hastened my departure from Toronto to Orangeville. On my arrival I at once located on a Clergy Reserve lot of land, on the first concession of the township of Amaranth, near Orangeville. As there was considerable demand for whiskey, I concluded to try another barrel, and accordingly took a yoke of oxen and went to Erin Village and purchased a fifty-two gallon barrel. The roads were bad, the snow being almost gone, nothing remaining but a bed of ice; and before I could descend the hills in Caledon I was compelled to cut places in the ice, where the oxen might get a foothold. No one but those who have had a similar experience can realize the difficulties of that trip. On my arrival at Orangeville —then a hamlet of three houses, but at the time of writing (1876) one of the most flourishing inland towns in Ontario, the junction of the two branches of the Toronto, Grey and Bruce Railroad, and containing a population of over three thousand inhabitants—I sold fully one-half my barrel of whiskey, and the remainder I soon after disposed of, a part of which has not yet been paid for. The first chopping I had attempted was on my new farm, and while underbrushing cut my foot severely, which laid me up for six weeks. Snow at that time fell to an average depth of about four feet in the bush; hence the toil, fatigue, and discomforts of chopping under such circumstances are incomprehensible to the uninitiated.

At this time I contracted no store debts, and thus avoided many of the troubles which harassed my neighbours. I went to the older settlements during haying and harvest, and with my earnings purchased such necessaries as were absolutely required ; and when a want occurred where the means were not available to meet it, I practised self-denial. Although I make no pretension to a greater share of worldly wisdom than the majority of my fellow-men, yet I believe few will dispute my assertion when I state that nine-tenths of the financial ills that have beset the first settlers throughout Canada may be traced to the facility with which they could become involved in debt, which hung like a millstone around their necks for a number of years, until, finally, either their energies became wasted so that they were no longer able to stem the current of compound interest, or their creditors sent in the sheriff to close the scene—the actors in the " Comedy of Errors " removing to another new section of country to conclude the farce of " Hewers of Wood and Drawers of Water." I had succeeded in clearing sufficient ground in the spring to sow a considerable area of wheat, besides a share of planted crop. The season was unpropitious, and my wheat was frozen so badly that I did not realize from my crop the quantity of seed I had sown.

The second year my grain was remarkably good, which awakened within me an inconceivable impulse in the performance of my arduous duties. With the first sleighing, myself and a neighbour, Mr. Christopher Irwin, each started with a small "grist" (the usual term applied to a quantity of grain milled for family use), and went to McLaughlin's mill, Mono Village. The night was stormy, and we remained till the morning. When about ready to start, I went to the only hotel in the village for a bottle of whiskey to treat the miller, Michael McLaughlin, Mr. Dodds, also an acquaintance, Mr. Irwin and myself. My bags, containing the proceeds of eight bushels of wheat, were standing not far from the door of the mill; but to my surprise, on returning, the grist was gone, "bag and baggage." One thing I was assured of, neither Mr. Irwin nor Mr. Dodds took it; and the only supposititious idea I entertain on the subject is, that the relative fairies of the McLaughlins had followed them from Ireland—for I often there heard they were great meal thieves—and spirited away my flour, shorts, bran, bags and all. Whether it was a knowledge of this fact that pricked the conscience of the honest miller, Mick McLaughlin, he reimbursed me with a generous donation of *ninety* pounds of very black flour. My expectations of the manner in which they "did things in the country" were considerably damped by this specimen of legerdemain, and caused me to sigh for the happy days I spent on my loom in

Ireland, with its witches, warlocks, fairies and all. The disappointment of my wife found expression in the remark that I had scarcely got the "toll," and lost the "grist."

The following year my grain crop was excellent, and I had no reason to complain of Amaranth ; but the Toronto line through the County of Grey being then recently surveyed, and the reports of the new settlers representing it as a second Garden of Eden, I with many others came to see it. The prospect was lovely ; where the surface was not covered with ground-hemlock, there was an abundance of wild nettles, cow cabbage, wild onions (leeks), &c., which certainly gave the virgin forest a luxuriant appearance. The black flies and mosquitoes assailed one in myriads, coming through the Township of Melancthon especially ; but even these torments seem frivolous when you "get used to it." There were three of us in company when we started to select a farm apiece. The three of us had made up our minds as to possessing *two* lots, and the difficulty arose how to decide. I agreed to "cast lots," but one of my companions refused to accede to that proposal; hence my other companion and myself became the possessors of the coveted lands—not that they turned out to be superior to thousands of acres in the same Township of Artemesia. The conditions of purchase were either immediate settlement, or "to be and appear once in each month on the said premises," with a view to making improvements thereon. This regulation led me to to make some twelve or thirteen trips through the Melancthon swamps before I finally settled down, at which time

I had a small clearing and a considerable quantity of potatoes and turnips raised. At this time it was impossible to work in small clearings without a veil to keep the flies away; and after four o'clock in the afternoon a "smudge" or slow fire had to be kindled to raise smoke to drive them away.

Late in the fall of this year, while still residing in Amaranth, I one night dreamed that a black man was seizing me, as if by authority, and in my fright woke up. At that instant I heard the squeal of a pig, six of which I had in an enclosure close to the dwelling. Jumping out of bed I seized a long-handled spade and rushed out, when there was a huge bear, with a pig in his arms, making his way out of the pig-sty. I struck him a blow with the spade, which broke the handle, causing Bruin to let go his hold of the pig, and I hastily entered the house, and through the window had the satisfaction of seeing the bear march slowly away without his prey. There were six large pigs in the "pen," and in the morning not one of them was to be seen; but a few days afterwards I found five of them some three miles distant, and on the eleventh day the one which had been in the tender embrace of the bear came back, dragging its hind-quarters on the ground, and a large "flake" of flesh, as large as my two outstretched hands, torn off the shoulder. With a patch of cloth torn off an old pair of canvas pants which I had worn in my sailor days, and a plentiful coating of melted pitch, I bound up the wound, and the pig (which was a female) I afterwards sold to Mr. John Mackay, of this township (Artemesia), who raised several litters of young from her.

I soon after this sold my place in Amaranth to Mr. John Armstrong, of the east of Munro, for forty dollars, an amount which at this day would seem inconsiderably small.

On the 14th February, 1851, I hired a team, bade adieu to Amaranth, and started for Artemesia. The snow was very deep, and we were two days travelling forty-four miles. From the Toronto line back to the next concession to my lot, there had been no traffic whatever, and the snow was on an average four feet deep; but with this difference from the snows of the present day, there were no drifts, owing to the universal shelter of the forest on every side.

I had brought with me a year's provisions, which lasted me till the growth of my own crop the following summer. I also brought a yoke of steers, two cows, a heifer, and some pigs. Fodder was almost out of the question, and I barely succeeded in purchasing two hundred pounds of straw, giving each animal a small handful night and morning, the rest of their subtenance depending entirely on browse; and although there were over two months of winter remaining, the cattle were in excellent condition in the spring. Of the two hundred pounds of straw, I had enough left in spring to fill a straw bed-tick for a neighbour. My first crop was excellent, and altogether the prospect in my new home was cheering.

I might here mention that in the early part of the winter I removed from Amaranth. I had been living alone in Artemesia, some nights remaining in my shanty, and at other times coming out to Mr. John May's. On one occasion while asleep in my shanty, I was awakened by some noise, and what was my surprise to see a large animal standing by the bedside, which I took to be a grey wolf. My terror was inexpressible. Perceiving that it made no demonstration such as might be expected from a ravenous wolf, upon closer examination I discerned that my self-invited guest was a large spotted dog. I was the only settler on the back line east of the Toronto and Sydenham road, and as there were no tracks of the dog having come from the front, the only conclusion I could satisfactorily arrive at was, that the dog belonged to some hunter, and that, while in pursuit of game, he had got out of reach of his master, and mine being the nearest habitation to the settlements on the north, his dogship paid me the visit in question. He stayed with me all day, and in the evening came with me to the front road, when he looked up in my face with an intelligent expression, and quietly trotted away in the direction of Owen Sound. At this time wolves were numerous, and in the summer bears were frequently met with.

Cattle-hunting, as the term goes, afforded many illustrations of "roughing it in the bush." Cattle would stray two, three and four miles back into the bush; and although that distance seems but trifling in the imagination, or through a cleared country, the reality of that distance in a dense forest of nightland, interspersed with swamps, marshes, beaver-meadows and jungles, is a different matter. In case the cattle were lying, the bells they carried would not be heard at times more than three or four hundred yards. Until a person became acquainted with the different swamps, beaver-meadows, &c., which served as landmarks, the most expert bushmen were sometimes at a loss to determine their position after running hither and thither for a few hours, especially if the day were cloudy. However, there was no difficulty in getting home if the cattle were found, for they could steer a straight line for home from any point they might be. Frequently, on my travels through the bush, when doubtful of my locality, I broke down small twigs and branches of trees, so that I might be able to retrace my steps; but frequently following these practices in the same locality rather tended to distract than to guide.

During the first year many persons were obliged to carry flour on their backs from the Township of St. Vincent, a distance of from fifteen to twenty-five miles. Every necessary of life was procurable only at an enormous sacrifice of toil and privation. The first flour I milled was made at a mill near Orangeville, a distance of forty-six miles. To the young man of to-day, that distance would seem a very long way, even with good roads and horse teams; but when bad roads, deep snows, and ox teams are taken into consideration, the magnitude of the task may be to some extent comprehended.

The second year brought about nothing worthy of special notice. Frost was unknown, except on very low lands. Late in the fall of the year, myself and Messrs. Peter Rowe, Wm. Bowler, Edward Fagan and Joseph Price, each started with our oxen and sleds and a small grist of wheat, for Walter's Falls mills, a distance of some eleven miles. There was no snow when going, but early on the following morning there was a depth of six or eight inches, and snow falling rapidly. Three of us took the route by seventy sideroad, thinking by that means to have a greater share of better road on the Toronto line ; the other two teams came by the Euphrasia and Holland town line. Before we reached the Toronto line the snow was between four and five feet deep, and towards evening the cold became intense. Our oxen were exhausted, and if one team remained ten minutes behind another, the track was filled up, the snow was falling so fast. What with breaking the road ahead of the oxen and the exertion required to wade through the deep snow, I was in a perspiration when we reached the Toronto line, where the road was much better. The slow pace of the oxen prevented me taking sufficient exercise to keep up warmth, and I became chilled, then benumbed, and finally, when I reached the foot of the hill on which Mr. John Allan's hotel stands, I was unable to walk, and crawled on my hands and knees most of the way up the hill. I was taken into Mr. Allan's and kindly cared for. My boots were frozen to my feet, so that they had to be thawed before they could be drawn off, and my right foot found badly frozen. I was compelled to remain two days before I was able to set out for home. My companions were nearly in as bad plight as myself.

The two who came by the town line had as much difficulty as ourselves. Mr. Bowler, being hindmost, had a narrow escape ; his oxen " gave out" and lay down, and he lay down, stretched between the two oxen, and thinks he may have lain about an hour, although he was only semi-conscious at the time, as he was so exhausted that he expected to die there. In a short time, however, the oxen arose, and aroused him, and they being refreshed, brought him home with little difficulty.

During the same day my wife went to the store of Mr. R. Lever, and when returning, worn out with cold and fatigue, called into the house of Mr. Alexander Madill, who loaned her a pair of drawers, which enabled her to reach home in safety.

I make this slight digression to illustrate the difficulties and dangers the first settlers encountered. My own experience in this respect is that of hundreds of others; and that many did not succumb in death when exposed to the rigours of winter, imperfectly clothed and scantily fed, seems almost miraculous.

In summer many families cked out an existence in a very precarious manner. In the early part of the summer, wild leeks and cow-cabbage, wild nettles, &c., were a valuable substitute for a more substantial meal. As soon as potatoes were the size of musket bullets they were carefully extracted from the root without injuring the stalk.

During the first years of my residence in Artemesia, myself and many of my neighbours went to the older settlements in haying and harvest, returning before our own crop was ripe. A portion of our earnings had to be carefully hoarded to meet the taxes, for it was next to impossible to obtain a cash market for farm produce nearer than Owen Sound.

I have also been to Owen Sound with a grist, and been

compelled to remain there three days and nights, sleeping in the mill at night, neither eating a warm meal from leaving home until my return, for the very good reason that I had no money. On one occasion I took a large load of wheat to Owen Sound market, which I sold to Mr. A. Neelands at the rate of 2s. 1d. (42 cents) per bushel. I purchased a Family Bible and a shawl for my wife, which left me five dollars in debt besides the proceeds of my load of wheat. In the following year (1854 –55) produce was somewhat enhanced in value owing to the Crimean war and the construction of the Grand Trunk Railway; still we were far in the back-ground, owing to the long distance from market—Owen Sound being the principal market of this county. Owing to the almost impassable state of the roads in the fall of the year, it was out of the question to forward grain in time for shipment before the close of navigation, and consequently where the grain had to be held over till spring, merchants could not give nearly as good prices as though they could forward it immediately to head-quarters. At the time of writing things have changed—a market at our own door—the sound of railway and steam whistles, of mills and manufactories, where a few short years ago resounded the howl of the wolf. Innumerable villages, containing mills, manufactories and general stores of merchandize now mark the spot which was overgrown by dense forest trees fifteen or twenty years ago. The stride of prosperity made by the County of Grey, and indeed the country at large, has been gigantic ; and it is a source of extreme gratification to me, as it no doubt will be to all the pioneers of my early days, that their sacrifice of worldly comforts and exposure to toil and suffering have so largely contributed to the development of our country and the welfare of succeeding generations.

The tendency of frost during the later years of settlement in this country is somewhat singular, as it is the general opinion that as a country becomes cleared, the frost decreases; but the history of this section of country proves the reverse. In the latter part of July, 1860, this section of country, as well as North America generally, was visited by a severe frost, which left many families destitute of bread for the succeeding winter. Some of my own wheat was so far advanced toward maturity that it escaped harm, but some spring wheat was totally destroyed. In the beginning of August this year my wife died, and nine days afterwards my youngest child, three years of age, also died—in both cases after a short illness. These sudden bereavements preyed heavily upon my mind, rendering me gloomy and spiritless in the prosecution of my labours; and as a consequence my affairs did not prosper. In about a year afterwards I again married, and have reason to look back with thankfulness upon the step I then took.

In June, 1864, this country was visited by a severe frost, which stunted meadow-grass and grain crops, the succeeding month being unusually dry, so that mowing hay or cradling grain was next to impossible, owing to the shortness of the crop. During this summer occurred the longest period of dry weather without rainfall within my recollection in Canada—the only period coming near to it being the summer of 1843.

One morning, in the commencement of my early settlement here, I went to search for my cattle, and had just caught sound of the bell, when three deer came galloping toward me. Those who have never seen wild deer in full flight through the forest, can form no conception of their majestic appearance and graceful motion, undulating beneath overhanging branches, or bounding over fallen timber six and even eight feet in height. I was intently gazing after their retreating forms, when my attention was attracted by a rustling sound behind me, and on turning round beheld a large grey wolf a few yards distant. He, too, was standing looking at me. He was soon joined by another, and in a few moments by two more. I concluded that " my hour had come." As domesticated dumb animals are said to seek protection from human beings in cases of danger, I reversed the rule, and ran toward my cattle, shouting at the top of my voice. The wolves followed on the track of the deer, probably as much astonished at my presence as I was frightened at theirs.

In the summer of 1863 occurred the election of George Jackson and George Snider. On the day previous to the " Declaration," five others besides myself started in a one-horse waggon to attend the demonstration. The horse was high-tempered, and at times difficult to manage. When going down the hill below the Orange Hall in Holland, on the Toronto and Sydenham Road, the horse began to plunge forward violently, and commenced to run away, all my efforts to restrain him being of no avail. Three of the company besides myself threw ourselves out of the waggon; the two others, Thos. Kells and Thos. Lackey,

4

were thrown out. Mr. Kells escaped with a few scratches, but poor Lackey fell with his head upon a stone. He was insensible when taken up ; but after we conveyed him to the house of Mr. John Martin, he became somewhat conscious. Dr. McGregor, of Johnstown, was sent for, but he was engaged in the election affairs, and it was the evening of the following day when Dr. Mahaffy arrived. He pronounced the skull broken, but that he was past cure, and the poor fellow breathed his last on the following day. His genial manners endeared him to a large circle of friends, and his untimely death cast an overshadowing gloom over the community.

This summer I had a narrow escape from being killed by a vicious bull I possessed. On several occasions he exhibited symptoms of a desire to attack me when I entered the enclosure of about a quarter of an acre in which he was kept. I determined to overawe him, and for that purpose entered the enclosure with a pitchfork in my hand ; and when he commenced brandishing his horns and pawing the earth with his feet, I gave him a slight probe with the prongs, when the brute charged, caught me upon his horns and tossed me into the air to a great height. I fell in a slight depression in the ground, which partially saved me from further attack, until the arrival of my son with the dog, which distracted the animal's attention until I had time to get over the fence out of his reach. My injuries were not severe, although I felt the effects of my "elevation" for some weeks afterwards.

In the year 1870 I met with another severe accident. A friend named James Brady came to visit me. I had put his horses in the stable, and when on the loft putting down some hay to them, I fell through the opening, alighting on the edge of the plank forming the manger, breaking two of my ribs, and otherwise bruising myself internally, the effects of which I feel to this day.

Time passed along with its usual ups and downs until December, when the agitation arose for the construction of the Toronto, Grey and Bruce Railroad from Orangeville to Owen Sound. The project was successful, and its construction has developed our County more during the two and a half years since it has been constructed than it progressed for fifteen years previously.

I might have devoted a portion of this work to writing a " Chapter of Accidents," as I have had a large share of these comforts. On the 23rd December, 1873, I went to assist my neighbour William Bowler in threshing. The day was stormy, with a head wind ; and although most of the men as well as myself desired to leave off till the following day, yet Mrs. B. put in a veto and the work continued. I was placed at the rear of the machine, and when we came to clean up the floor—the accumulated dust, thistle-downs, and other accumulations of dust and dirt— the dust blinded me so that when I went out of the barn, not being able to see the danger, I stepped close to the " knuckle " of the tumbling-shaft, which caught my pants, and drew my leg and body around with it in its course. I had sufficient presence of mind to throw myself at full length upon the shaft, grasping it with my arms, otherwise I must inevitably have been crushed to death. As it was, my body was whirled round and round, the space between the shaft and solid earth being only six inches. My right foot and leg were almost powerless, and my right arm was broken in two places—above and below the elbow—and it was, as well as my right leg, twisted round the shaft in such a manner that the latter had to be turned in a reverse direction before I could be extricated. The threshing machine might have been stopped sooner had it not been that there was neither a sheaf of grain or bundle of straw to choke the cylinder; but, with admirable forethought, Mr. Gilbert, who was "feeding," threw in his wool hat, which almost stopped it. My head was bruised in a shocking manner; my forehead was devoid of feeling to the touch during the next three or four weeks. I was carried into the house, and soon afterwards drawn home in a sleigh. I was so much broken and bruised that my clothing could not be removed, and was put to bed in the clothing I had worn at the threshing, the barley beards, thistles and chaff they contained making it very uncomfortable. In this position I was compelled to lie for fifteen weeks. Dr. Sproule attended me. As my nerves began to regain their sensitiveness, the agony of my situation increased proportionately. There seemed to be ten thousand thistles in my clothing, each of them "right end up," but not "with care." I had read the figurative description of lying on a bed of thorns, but I never till then fully realized the full import of the parable. The day seemed to be never-ending, and the night without a dawn.

However, everything will have an end, and so did my illness. My leg, as I previously remarked, was powerless. This was not so much to be wondered at: the sinews and muscles had been ruptured, so that to place them in their former positions would have been simply impossible ; but my arm was twisted, in being set, at the break above the elbow ; consequently there was a "hitch" at this place, which turned my hand half round, and rendered my arm comparatively useless. Dr. Sproule was the first person who raised me out of bed, and I was so weak that I had not been raised up on the bedside more than two minutes before I fainted. I was many times raised before I could bear the fatigue more than two or three minutes, so weak had I become.

I went to Toronto to see if anything could be done to put me in more possession of the use of my arm. Several eminent surgeons to whom I applied informed me that as I was aged, and having already undergone so much suffering, it was questionable whether I would be able to sustain this second shock to my nervous system. This, I believe, was correct, for I could not take a drink of cold water without producing a stinging pain between my eyes and in my forehead, so sensitive and weak had my nerves become. Dr. Aikins, of the Toronto Hospital, proposed to place me under the influence of chloroform, break my arm over again, set it right, and assured me he would "set me all right in nine days ;" but I had suffered so much in the past, and although assured there would be no consciousness of pain on my part, I dreaded the ordeal of breaking newly-knit bones, and concluded to suffer the consequences of my misfortune. I afterwards applied to Dr. Edgar, of Yorkville, who rendered me considerable benefit. He gave me some medicine to take inwardly, which renovated my nervous system, and prescribed the daily use of cold water poured upon my spine every morning. This I followed for some time, and felt a beneficial influence upon my right leg; but the cold weather was coming on, and not having a suitable room in which to use this application, it was discontinued.

After my first experience on being taken up out of bed, I had to be kept in bed fully a week before I could be raised a second time, but was occasionally raised with pillows; and when taken out of bed, had to be placed in a rocking-chair and drawn across the floor—this continued for two or three weeks—and then led by the arm: a true phase of second childhood.

From that time forward I continued to gain strength. I hired a man to assist in working my farm; but as I found this unprofitable, the cost overrunning the profit, I concluded to sell my farm and seek to earn my livelihood and provide for my family in some mode in which physical exertion would not be so much called into requisition as it was on the farm.

Accordingly I sold my farm, and opened a small store in the Village of Markdale, where I now reside; and although each day of my life reminds me *painfully* of my infirmities, yet my natural buoyancy of spirits keeps me consoled, and activity of mind prevents me, in a great measure, experiencing the loss of my limbs. Being in very moderate circumstances, a less sanguine temperament would have succumbed to the deprivation; but, with a firm faith in the truth of the moral which teaches that "God helps those who help themselves," I have written this sketch of my life, in the hope that those who purchase it may be benefited by reading its contents, and that it may contribute to the publisher his due reward.

Before parting with the reader, I wish to say that I have not penned these lines as a masterpiece of composition—this has not been my aim—but I have exhibited my own life, with all its imperfections, as a guide to the reader in the path of his own journey through life. As I said in the former part of this work, I received little book or school education; but my mature judgment convinces me that book learning is only an *aid* to a true education. The multitude of my fellow-men think that education consists in loading a child's mind with a given number of words from a Walker's, Johnson's, or Webster's Dictionary, with a corresponding quantity of figures, to prepare for the routine of trade. Writing is but an instrument—a mere mechanical operation. But I hold that the true end of a sound education is the acquisition of the power of thought—power to gain happiness from, and contribute happiness to, all those with whom our presence comes in contact. Education should be so directed that it would enable us to draw correct premises from the past, and discover the source of a false judgment. This I hold to be an essential part of a good education. The mind was not created to receive passively a number of "set" lessons, to develop into that maturity which should shed lustre upon the human family in the sight of the Creator, but that which expands the mind into a desire for the acquirement of Truth. Accordingly, a true education should inspire us with a profound love of truth, and teach us that *honour*, not *talents*, make the true gentleman. Let the thought, however, not be entertained for one moment that I depreciate book learning—it is that which exalts youth, conveys wisdom to the mature, and lends comfort to the aged. In the performance of its task it fears no dangers; it penetrates the bowels of the earth; explores sea and land; dives to the depths of the ocean; ascends to the sublime. No worlds too remote for its grasp; no heavens too exalted for its reach.

www.ingramcontent.com/pod-product-compliance
Lightning Source LLC
Chambersburg PA
CBHW051735020426
42333CB00014B/1316